Author: Todd Palmer
Editor: Jeanette Micallef

ISBN: 150601075X
ISBN-13: 978-1506010755

WELCOME

Welcome to The Job Search Process™.
This book represents the culmination of
everything I have learned from a
successful career helping people just
like you find and land the jobs they want
and need. I guarantee that if you follow
this course to the letter, in just 6 weeks
you'll be celebrating YOUR new job, and
all the wonderful benefits that come
along with that success.

Let's get started!

TABLE OF CONTENTS

1. Prepare for your Job Search

2. Create a Quality Resume and Cover Letter

3. Locate and Apply for Job Opportunities

4. Interview Prep

5. Ace your Interview

6. Follow Up

7. When, What and How to Negotiate

8. Start Your New Job with a Bang!

9. Bonus Step: The Last-Ditch Effort
   (Recommended for Dream Jobs Only)

PREPARE FOR YOUR JOB SEARCH

Landing a job takes nothing more than salesmanship. To be successful, you'll need to be able to sell yourself and your skills to another person. Before you can do this, you'll need to be an expert on what it is you're selling.

You'll need to figure a few things out first:

- **Who are you, really, and what do you have to offer a new company?**
- **What are you looking for in your next job?**
- **What will you need to do to get that job, and can you commit to doing whatever it takes?**

The first step in the Job Search Process™ is to learn about yourself and your situation. You'll have to take an objective look at both these things in order to answer those questions, but once you do, you'll be ready to tackle anything your job search throws at you!

GET REAL

Most people have blind spots when it comes to looking at themselves, their skillsets, and their job expectations. It is common for people to feel bitter about things in their lives that haven't turned out the way they had envisioned. Jobs are closely tied to our identity, and often have a great impact on our self-worth.

As you begin to look at yourself and your situation, see if you have any feelings of resentment toward others, or struggles you may have with self-confidence based on your current job situation. If so, consider getting some help to break yourself out of that negative cycle.

 Create a support system for yourself during this job search journey — talk to your family, friends, clergy, or a job coach. Avoid people who might push you back toward the negative.

Sometimes friends and family will try to show support by taking your side and insisting you were cheated out of something at your last job, or that your next boss "owes" you something. This is a good time to let them know that the best support is positive comments and encouragement. If they cannot adjust their means of support, you may need to steer clear of them for a while. It is important to surround yourself with people who lift you up, not hold you back. Dwelling on the past, and previous expectations will only hinder your search. You are out to find a job. Be optimistic. Have a positive attitude. Focus on the future.

DUMP YOUR EGO

Life is tough. It's just a fact. Blaming your old boss for your current situation won't change anything, and replaying thoughts over and over in your head will do nothing but make you miserable.

I once knew someone who thought that if he just got a degree, he would be able to break out of retail, and land himself a white collar management job. So he went back to school and got his degree, but his job didn't change. Instead of working to change his situation, he blamed the school where he got his degree.

Refusing to take responsibility for his situation, he became so bitter and angry at the school that he couldn't focus on anything else. His vicious cycle of negative thoughts has him still working at the same retail store, and he's still miserable.

Sometimes it's hard to keep our egos in check, but this kind of mindset actually prevents us from seeing circumstances the way they really are. Rather than laying blame, it's important to remain objective, and open to new possibilities. Learn to be open to help from others, and accept it with gratitude. Be willing to work hard and take control of your job future.

BRACE YOURSELF FOR AN EMOTIONAL ROLLERCOASTER

Every job seeker goes through highs and lows in the process. You'll likely experience many of these different stages. Try to get through many of them as quickly as possible.

Choose to learn and grow from your experiences instead of panicking about them.

Stage 1:   Focused/Positive
What you feel: As a new job seeker, you're focused on the Job Search Process™, sending positive messages to the brain, like, "I can do this!"
What to do: Try to stay in this stage as long as possible.

Stage 2:   Frustration
What you feel: Obstacles will pop up. Interviews may not happen. Other people will get jobs before you.
What to do: Focus on your search, not on other people around you. Each day is one step closer to getting your next job.

Stage 3:   Shock

What you feel: You can't believe you're still looking. They said the job search thing would be so easy!

What to do: Review your tracking form. Where you are looking? What are you doing? Identify patterns of what is working and what isn't.

Stage 4:   Denial

What you feel: Withdrawal from Job Search Process™, marked by procrastination, not following up, and eating and sleeping a lot!

What to do: Ask friends and family for support. Exercise. Walk the dog, take a run, or job hunt in a new location for a fresh start.

Stage 5:   Fear

What you feel: Negative thoughts will begin to creep in, "I can't do this, I'll never find a job," or "The world is against me!"

What to do: Keep in mind that you are in control of your thoughts, your feelings, and in turn, your actions. Like the band, Sister Hazel sings, "If you want to be somebody else, change your mind." It's not just a catchy tune, it's the truth.

Stage 6:   Anger Part 1

What you feel: You begin to blame everyone else. You wonder, "Why weren't they honest with me?" or think, "They lied to me!"

Stage 7:   Anger Part 2

What you feel: You get angry with yourself.

What to do: Acknowledge your feelings. Take full responsibility for your life and your choices.

You may have days where you find yourself back at Stage 1, or bouncing between stages. This is normal. Stay positive. Be realistic. Keep your goals in mind and don't get discouraged.

CONSIDER CHANGING CAREERS

It's a little known fact that the average American changes careers, not just jobs, six times in their lifetime, roughly every four years. You are not alone. Others have traveled this path before you.

If your old job has disappeared, it's time to consider what else you're good at, or how your existing skills may apply to a new job. It is key to know that the skills you already have can be used in different areas, and you'll need to learn how to market them to potential employers.

Complete the Transferable Skills Checklist on the next few pages to get a good look at your options. You just might learn something!

TRANSFERABLE SKILLS CHECKLIST

You have developed many skills over the years working other jobs, attending school, participating in social activities and volunteer work, and by simply living your life.

If you have done research, written a report, or edited and presented papers for a class, you have used skills that are transferable to many different occupations or disciplines.

A prospective employer expects you to be able to apply the skills you have learned in college to the work environment. Use the following checklist to help you pinpoint some of your transferable skills.

COMMUNICATION SKILLS
___ speaking effectively
___ writing clearly and concisely
___ listening attentively and objectively
___ expressing ideas
___ facilitating group discussion
___ interviewing
___ editing
___ responding appropriately to +/- feedback
___ using various media to present ideas imaginatively
___ providing appropriate feedback
___ negotiating
___ perceiving non-verbal messages
___ persuading
___ reporting information
___ describing feelings
___ public speaking
___ using various styles of written communication
___ conveying a positive self-image to others

RESEARCH / PLANNING / INVESTIGATING
___ forecasting / predicting

___ creating ideas
___ identifying problems
___ imagining alternatives
___ identifying resources
___ gathering information
___ solving problems
___ setting goals
___ extracting important information
___ analyzing
___ developing evaluation strategies
___ testing validity of data
___ designing an experiment or model
___ formulating questions
___ making conclusions
___ conceptualizing
___ observing

HUMAN RELATIONS / INTERPERSONAL
___ developing rapport
___ being sensitive
___ listening
___ conveying feelings
___ providing support for others
___ motivating

TRANSFERABLE SKILLS CHECKLIST

HUMAN RELATIONS / INTERPERSONAL *(cont.)*

___ sharing credit
___ helping others
___ counseling
___ cooperating
___ keeping a group "on track"
___ being patient
___ interacting effectively with peers, superiors and subordinates
___ persuading others
___ being willing to take risks
___ teaching / instructing others
___ demonstrating effective social behavior
___ perceiving feelings and situations
___ delegating with respect
___ working with diversity or multi-cultural issues

WORK SURVIVAL

___ implementing decisions
___ cooperating
___ enforcing policies
___ being punctual
___ managing time and stress
___ attending to detail
___ working effectively under pressure
___ taking initiative in job-related duties
___ discerning appropriate behaviors for the workplace
___ meeting goals
___ enlisting help
___ accepting responsibility
___ setting and meeting deadlines
___ organizing
___ making decisions
___ seeking opportunities for professional development
___ evaluating personal and professional strengths and weaknesses

ORGANIZATION / MANAGEMENT / LEADERSHIP / DECISION MAKING

___ initiating new ideas and tasks
___ handling details
___ coordinating tasks
___ coaching / mentoring

___ counseling
___ managing conflict
___ motivating and leading people
___ organizing people and tasks to achieve a specific goal
___ following up with others to evaluate progress
___ conducting meetings
___ giving praise and credit to others for a job well done
___ negotiating agreements
___ taking responsibility for decisions

FINANCIAL MANAGEMENT

___ developing a budget accurately estimating expenses and income
___ keeping accurate and complete financial records
___ accounting
___ assessing
___ ensuring timeliness of payments
___ fundraising
___ calculating
___ projecting / forecasting
___ investing

CRITICAL THINKING / PROBLEM SOLVING

___ anticipating problems before they occur
___ defining problems and identifying possible causes
___ identifying possible solutions and selecting the most appropriate ones
___ creating innovative solutions to complex problems
___ involving group members to evaluate solutions
___ developing plans to implement solutions
___ multi-tasking
___ identifying a general principle that explains interrelated experience

PUTTING YOUR TRANSFERABLE SKILLS TO WORK

List five skills that you consider your best transferable skills. Write an example of where or how you have used each skill, and rank the skills 1-5, with 1 being the most important.

RANK: SKILL:

EXAMPLE:

RANK: SKILL:

EXAMPLE:

RANK: SKILL:

EXAMPLE:

RANK: SKILL:

EXAMPLE:

RANK: SKILL:

EXAMPLE:

Note: This skillset list is provided to give you ideas for how to develop your own list of skills, in your own writing style. On a resume, skills should always be used in conjunction with specific job duties or responsibilities. A listing of skills without further explanation should only occur in the "summary" section of your resume.

You might even consider going back to school or getting more training. If so, look into the "No Worker Left Behind" program in your state.

TAKE OWNERSHIP OF YOUR JOB SEARCH

Be empowered and in control of your job future! The fact is, when it comes to finding a job, no one can do the work for you. Having a family member "pull some strings" no longer works. Competition is too great for that. The responsibility of getting a job is yours. You need to believe in yourself, and make it happen.

Try to visualize the outcome. Stop for a moment. Close your eyes. Imagine the pride you will feel walking into your next job. Can you see that smile on your face? That spring in your step?

Now promise yourself a reward for the day that you make that happen. For example, dinner at your favorite upscale restaurant, a new dress, or maybe something as simple as going to the theater for a movie you have been wanting to see.

If you are finding it difficult to feel positive and empowered, begin reading any of the following motivational books to shake yourself from your funk:

- *The Power of Positive Thinking*, by Dr. Norman Vincent Peale
- *The Success Principals*, by Jack Canfield
- *The Secret*, by Rhonda Byrne
- *How to Get What You Want and Want What You Have*, by John Gray
- *Awaken the Giant Within*, by Tony Robbins
- *Thinking For a Change*, by John C. Maxwell

If you like physical activity, try jogging, walking, or yoga. The positive chemical release within your brain can help get you moving in the right direction to find your next job.

BE SOMEONE THEY WANT TO BE AROUND

Ultimately, the bottom line is that managers hire people they like and want to be around. The single most important thing I have learned in my 12+ years as a recruiter and job seeker, is that managers will hire someone they like over an equally qualified candidate they don't like — every time.

As a general rule, no one wants to work with someone they don't like or someone who gives a bad first impression. People don't usually choose to surround themselves with negative or self-centered people. Make the decision to be positive and enthusiastic, and to attract others with your charm. Commit to that mentality and watch it actually work!

GETTING TO KNOW YOU

Getting to know who you really are, and figuring out what you are capable of as a human being, can be challenging. As challenging as it can be, it is a crucial first step to beginning your job search process, and to knowing how to keep yourself focused and motivated while on the tough road ahead.

Knowing and believing that you are a worthwhile person, who can and will be a valued employee, is the best place to start. Now that you have gotten rid of all that negative junk that was in your head, refilled it with the positive stuff, and recognized that the Job Search Process™ is your journey to embark upon, it's time to create your paper announcement to the job world that you are qualified, motivated, and ready to make a difference for their business.

It is now time to create your resume!

CREATE A QUALITY RESUME & COVER LETTER

There are varying opinions on how to best write a resume. Some people think that the most important parts of the resume are the font, the color of the paper, and the layout. In all my years as a recruiter, I have learned that those things don't matter nearly as much as the content of the resume. When it comes to the format, don't overthink it.

At the end of the day, there are only two types of resumes that you need to consider, the chronological resume and the functional resume. They are both standard, globally acceptable resume formats. Let's review each type, and then you can decide which one works better for you. I have included several examples of each so you can see what they look like.

First, we will look at the chronological resume. Who should use this format?

- Recent high school or college graduates
- Someone with limited job experience
- Someone with steady work experience in their desired career field

Chronological resumes start by listing work history, with the most recent listed first. Jobs are listed in reverse order after the most current position. Employers prefer this format because it's easy to see what jobs you've held, how long you were there, and what you've accomplished.

For the recent college graduate looking for their first job, the chronological resume can indicate that the student, while in school full time, also held a part-time job. This shows an employer that the student has great time-management skills.

For the person who has held the same job for a significant amount of time, this format shows that the applicant is loyal, dedicated and can be a good asset to the corporation.

On the next few pages, you will find several chronological resume samples. Find the one that fits your personality and plug in your information. It's that easy!

Now, let's look at the functional resume. Who should use this format?

- Someone re-entering the workforce
- Someone interested in changing careers who wants to market their "transferable" skills
- Someone who has a done a tremendous amount of freelance or independent contractor work

The objective of this format is to focus on the applicant's skills and accomplishments. Be sure to include a listing of your employers.

As you get started on a functional resume, keep in mind that some employers to do not like this format, because it is easy to forget to include skills, levels of responsibility and dates of employment.

In the next pages, you will find two functional resume samples. Find the one that fits, and personalize it with your information.

CHRONOLOGICAL RESUME 1

John Doe
6 Pine Street
Arlington, VA 12333
Mobile (555) 444-5555
jdoe123@gmail.com

OBJECTIVE: Gain a full-time retail management position

EXPERIENCE:

Key Holder, Montblanc   **April 2001- February 2005**
•Opened new specialty boutique
•Placed orders to restock merchandise and handled receiving of products
•Managed payroll, scheduling, reports, email, inventory, and maintained clientele book and records
•Integrated new register functions
•Extensive work with visual standards and merchandising high-ticket items

Sales Associate, Nordstrom   **July 1999 – April 2001**
Collectors and Couture Departments
- Merchandised designer women's wear
- Set up trunk shows and attended clinics for new incoming fashion lines
- Worked with tailors and seamstresses for fittings
- Scheduled private shopping appointments with high-end customers

Bartender, Jigg's Corner   **February 1997 – July 1999**
- Provide customer service in fast-paced bar atmosphere
- Maintain and restock inventory
- Administrative responsibilities include processing hour and tip information for payroll and closing register
- Scheduled private shopping appointments with high-end customers

EDUCATION:

Ramapo College, Arlington, Virginia
Graduated 2001, B.S. Management

Computer Skills:

Proficient in Microsoft Word, Excel, PowerPoint, internet

CHRONOLOGICAL RESUME 2

Jane Doe
123 Main Street
Dayton, OH 48067
(555) 555-5555

OBJECTIVE: Obtain a full-time position as a Mechanical Engineer

ENGINEERING EXPERIENCE:

Industrial Engineer   1998
– 2007
Tool Incorporated, Warren, OH
- Designed a plant layout for the shipping department
- Developed a multi-step shipping process improvement plan

Design Engineer   1995 – 1998
Mechanical Systems, Columbus, OH
- Developed a complete safety package for a robot loader
- Designed hydraulic double stack lift
- Redesigned dairy open-style conveyor
- Trained 10 engineers on AutoCAD Rev. 12
- Evaluated and purchased machine components

HVAC Engineer Assistant   1990 – 1995
Engineering Consultants, Columbus, OH
- Prepared building and equipment
- Developed a multi-step shipping process improvement plan

MANAGEMENT EXPERIENCE:

Supervisor   1987
– 1990
College Police Department, Cincinnati, OH
- Supervised more than 50 student security personnel
- Maintained security accounts and budgets
- Interviewed, hired, field trained and conducted performance appraisals
- Prepared 25 page monthly reports

Manager   1987 – 1990
Building Management Company, Cincinnati, OH
- Maintained and performed building improvements

EDUCATION:

Bachelor of Science Degree: Mechanical Engineering   1990 – 1995
Minor: Engineering Management
University of Cincinnati, Cincinnati, OH

Computer Skills: AutoCAD 12, FORTRAN, Lotus and Quattro Pro, MS Office

FUNCTIONAL RESUME 1

JOHN DOE
1234 Circle Drive
Minneapolis, Minnesota 55404
(612) 555-5555

OBJECTIVE
Seeking a welding or building maintenance position.

SUMMARY OF QUALIFICATIONS

Welding—
Developed extensive experience in a wide variety of welding styles and positions including:

MIG	TIG	ARC
Heliarc		
Oxyacetylene	Air ARC	Cutting and Gouging
Automatic Seam		
Plasma Cutting	Underwater	Water-Cooled Spot Welding

Fabrication—
Skilled in layout and design of sheet metal and pipe. Developed extensive knowledge of sheet rollers and brakes. Followed Manufacturer's Operating Processes (MOP) to detail.

Equipment Operator—
Experienced forklift operator on various sized and styles of forklifts. Skilled in the use of a variety of power tools and metal fabrication equipment including: drills, drill press, edge planer, end mill, benders, power saws, sanders and grinders.

Equipment Maintenance—
Performed general maintenance on welding equipment and production machinery. Maintained high production levels through onsite machine repairs and preventative maintenance.

Building Maintenance—
Acquired experience in general construction including basic electrical repairs, carpentry, concrete, glass, spray and roller painting, plumbing, patching and sheetrock.

SUMMARY OF EXPERIENCE

Welding Inc., Minneapolis
Lead Welder (1997 – present)
- Maintained strict performance, quality and production standards
- Trained new employees and monitored their performance during probationary period

EDUCATION

Certificate:
Welding and Blueprint Reading
Minneapolis Community and Technical college – Minneapolis, MN (1997)

Diploma:
Central High School – Saint Paul, MN 1(995)

FUNCTIONAL RESUME 2

Kristen Taylor Allen
123 Paradise Way
Smooth Sailing, CA 12345-6789
Home: (123) 555-0221
Work: (123) 555-9083

OBJECTIVE

Administrative support position in a major marketing division; to use my clerical, organizational and planning experience.

EXPERIENCE
- Kept extensive, detailed records on several market research projects at one time.
- Edited, composed and word-processed all documents for these and for several others in development.
- Used responses to generate a $1.5 million ad campaign, which resulted in $5.5 million in new business.

ORGANIZATIONAL
- During extensive cutbacks and start of closure of bank's marketing department, reconfigured department for optimal operation.
- Helped create market research projects, restructured duties in department to accommodate each project.

PLANNING
- Suggested and implemented hire of research associates, data analysts and other specialists.
- Developed flex-time schedule for work to maximize use of office space during research projects.

EMPLOYMENT
- **1995-Present – Bilksteal Bankshares,** *Administrative Aide*
- **1992-1995 – Pack Advertising,** *Market Researcher*
- **1989-1992 – Quick Markets,** *Payroll Director*

SKILLS

Proficient on Hewlett-Packard D2-4000 Data Processor. Use Windows PC, Apple, Lotus and other specialized programs. Learn quickly. Solve problems efficiently.

EDUCATION

South Virginia community College, Associate in Secretarial Science, 1968, Cum Laude
American Banking Institute Coursework, 1977-1980
Southside University, courses in computer graphics and organizational behavior, 1989-1991

You've seen a couple of great examples of what chronological and functional resumes look like, now let's see what not to do. The truth is, employers see ten bad resumes for every good one. Don't let yourself be one of the ten! This resume has an unclear objective, is poorly laid out, and gives too much information about previous employers instead of listing responsibilities and accomplishments.

BAD RESUME 1

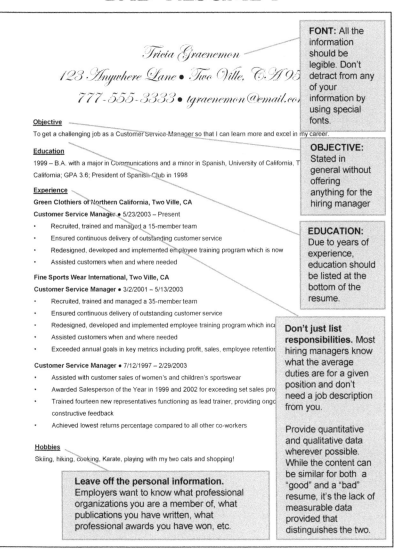

BAD RESUME 2

John Doe
555interview rd apt 2
any town mn 55111

11-4-05

Employment history:

mcdonalds: 1996-2001 burger flipper
Burger king 2001-2002 fry station

Education:

High school
No college

Reference:

Bob smith 612-555-1212
Todd Johnson: unknown
Chris adams: 612-555-4112 ?

Position applying for: manager

There are quite a few things wrong with this resume. Here are some of the basic things to change:

- **Address:** Do not abbreviate
- **Phone number:** make sure you have one listed.
- **Date:** Not necessary on a resume.
- **Employment:** List the title, dates of employment and describe each position.
- **Education:** List school name, location and graduation date. Do not list education you do not have.
- **References:** Do not include on resume.
- **Position applied for:** Do not include on resume, only in cover letter.
- **Capitalization:** Use when appropriate, such as names of businesses, addresses, cities.
- **Punctuation:** Use when appropriate, such as between city and state, between employer name and position held.
- **Spell Check:** Always, always spell check your resume.

BAD RESUME 3

> This resume is neither chronological nor functional in format. It combines a resume and a cover letter into a lengthy and conversational letter. It includes references (which should be provided later, upon request), does not list any dates, and is full of spelling mistakes.

Natalie Employee
123 Job Street
Workerville, New York 01236
(555) 555-5555

Objective: To get a good paying job

Education:

Worsh College of Business, Workerville, New York

I received my Associate Degree in Legal Administrative Assistant in August, 2002. During this time, I studies various subjects, which I did well in. Some of the computer skills that I am proficient in are Microsoft Office Suite, Word Perfect, and Desktop Publishing. I also did well in course work in the areas of Business Law, Accounting, Legal Office Systems, Information technology, and Composition and Research. I scored well on all exams, and feel that I am capable of working in these areas.

Work Skills/Duties I Have Performed

I have worked in the Legal Assistant/Secretarial field for several years. I have performed general legal office procedures, prepared legal documents, composed legal correspondence, prepared bank forms for mortgage closings and refinances, and performed title searches. I have handled general filing for a busy law office, operated a switchboard in a busy law office, and carried out other general reception duties as required.

I have also worked in customer service and fod service. In these areas, I have processed customer orders, handled the cash drawer, solved customer problems, prepared food for a busy sandwich shop, and performed general cleaning and maintenance duties. My employers told me that I was a very conscientious worker, and that they enjoyed having me on board.

Jobs/Work Experiences

Anderson, Bruford, Wakeman and Howe, LLP. Workerville, New York Legal Assitant

Law Offices of Attorney Cheryl L. Stein, Workerville, New York Legal Assistant

Jerry Seinfeld Law Offices, Workerville, New York Legal Assistant Intern

Bill and Ted's Sandwich Shop, Workerville, New York Customer Service/Food Prep

Burger King Carol's Corporation, Workerville, New York Cahier/Cook

In addition to these employers and experiences, I also have good references. I have included these references hear:

Joe Reference, Owner
Bill and Ted's Sandwich Shop Aunt
555-555-5555

Mary Reference

555-555-1234

Your resume needs to be clear and legible, but keep in mind that this is not a beauty pageant. Your resume doesn't have to look pretty for someone to take the time to read it. For someone like me, who reads an average of 100 resumes every day, I can tell you that the true beauty of the resume is not in the way it physically looks, but the story it tells and the details that it gives to the employer.

Nowadays, advances in technology have employers receiving more resumes than ever, including many from people who aren't even qualified for the particular job.

Standing out from the crowd requires creating a quality resume that speaks to your potential employer. A resume should focus on your accomplishments, to showcase the skills you can bring to the company.

One of the biggest mistakes that I see in resumes is listing all the responsibilities you've had at past jobs, instead of your accomplishments. That won't grab anyone's attention.

Potential employers can usually guess what your responsibilities were based on your job title. They don't want to know what you did from clock-in to clock-out. They want to know that you're a mover and a shaker – how you contributed to the organization, how you show initiative and leadership, how you made the company profitable, and that you can be a key player. That's what they want to see.

SELL YOURSELF WITH ACTION WORDS

Brag! Most resumes have too much fluff. Adding filler phrases just creates confusion and distraction. Filling your resume with fluff does not make it look bigger and better. Your resume needs strong action verbs describing what you have done and what you can do.

- If you have made process improvements in a manufacturing company—SAY IT!

- If you were in sales and increased profits—SAY IT!

- If you were in a clerical support position and came up with a better way to organize something or someone—SAY IT!

Forget what your parents taught you about not being a boaster or a braggart. Your resume is your individual sales brochure. If you don't tell the world how great you are, who will?

Following are suggested action words, listed by skill set, that will help make your resume shine:

Communication/People Skills

Addressed, Advertised, Arbitrated, Arranged, Articulated, Authored, Clarified, Collaborated, Communicated, Composed, Condensed, Conferred, Consulted, Contacted, Conveyed, Convinced, Corresponded, Debated, Defined, Developed, Directed, Discussed, Drafted, Edited, Elicited, Enlisted, Explained, Expressed, Formulated, Furnished, Incorporated, Influenced, Interacted, Interpreted, Interviewed, Involved, Joined, Judged, Lectured, Listened, Marketed, Mediated, Moderated, Negotiated, Observed, Outlined, Participated, Persuaded, Presented, Promoted, Proposed, Publicized, Reconciled, Recruited, Referred, Reinforced, Reported, Resolved, Responded, Solicited, Specified, Spoke, Suggested, Summarized, Synthesized, Translated, Wrote

Creative Skills

Acted, Adapted, Began, Combined, Composed, Conceptualized, Condensed, Created, Customized, Designed, Developed, Directed, Displayed, Drew, Entertained, Established, Fashioned, Formulated, Founded, Illustrated, Initiated, Instituted, Integrated, Introduced, Invented, Modeled, Modified, Originated, Performed, Photographed, Planned, Revised, Revitalized, Shaped, Solved Data/Financial Skills Administered, Adjusted, Allocated, Analyzed, Appraised, Assessed, Audited, Balanced, Budgeted, Calculated, Computed, Conserved, Corrected, Determined, Developed, Estimated, Forecasted, Managed, Marketed, Measured, Netted, Planned, Prepared, Programmed, Projected, Qualified, Reconciled, Reduced, Researched, Retrieved

Helping Skills
Adapted, Advocated, Aided, Answered, Arranged, Assessed, Assisted, Clarified, Coached, Collaborated, Contributed, Cooperated, Counseled, Demonstrated, Diagnosed, Educated, Encouraged, Ensured, Expedited, Facilitated, Familiarized, Furthered, Guided, Helped, Insured, Intervened, Motivated, Prevented, Provided, Referred, Rehabilitated, Represented, Resolved, Simplified, Supplied, Supported, Volunteered

Management/Leadership Skills
Administered, Analyzed, Appointed, Approved, Assigned, Attained, Authorized, Chaired, Considered, Consolidated, Contracted, Controlled, Converted, Coordinated, Decided, Delegated, Developed, Directed, Eliminated, Emphasized, Enforced, Enhanced, Established, Executed, Generated, Handled, Headed, Hired, Hosted, Improved, Incorporated, Increased, Initiated, Inspected, Instituted, Led, Managed, Merged, Motivated, Navigated, Organized, Originated, Overhauled, Oversaw, Planned, Presided, Prioritized, Produced, Recommended, Reorganized, Replaced, Restored, Reviewed, Scheduled, Secured, Selected, Streamlined, Strengthened, Supervised, Terminated

Organizational Skills
Approved, Arranged , Catalogued, Categorized, Charted, Classified Coded, Collected, Compiled, Corrected, Corresponded, Distributed, Executed, Filed, Generated, Incorporated, Inspected, Logged, Maintained, Monitored, Obtained, Operated, Ordered, Organized, Prepared, Processed, Provided, Purchased, Recorded, Registered, Reserved, Responded, Reviewed, Routed, Scheduled, Screened, Submitted, Supplied., Standardized, Systematized, Updated, Validated, Verified

Research Skills
Analyzed, Clarified, Collected, Compared, Conducted, Critiqued, Detected, Determined, Diagnosed, Evaluated, Examined , Experimented, Explored, Extracted, Formulated, Gathered, Inspected, Interviewed, Invented, Investigated, Located, Measured, Organized, Researched, Reviewed, Searched, Solved, Summarized, Surveyed, Systematized, Tested

Teaching Skills
Adapted, Advised, Clarified, Coached, Communicated, Conducted, Coordinated, Critiqued, Developed, Enabled, Encouraged, Evaluated, Explained, Facilitated, Focused, Guided, Individualized, Informed, Instilled, Instructed, Motivated, Persuaded, Simulated, Stimulated, Taught, Tested, Trained, Transmitted, Tutored

Technical Skills
Adapted, Applied, Assembled, Built, Calculated, Computed, Conserved, Constructed, Converted, Debugged, Designed, Determined, Developed, Engineered, Fabricated, Fortified, Installed, Maintained, Operated, Overhauled, Printed, Programmed, Rectified, Regulated, Remodeled, Repaired, Replaced, Restored, Solved, Specialized, Standardized, Studied, Upgraded, Utilized

FOCUS ON MEASURABLE RESULTS

Show results you can prove with numbers or facts. Companies will hire you if you have a skill that they need, and if they see that your goal is to help them fulfill that need by hiring you. Tell them exactly what your skills and talents are and how they benefited your previous employers. The more "measured out" data you provide, the more they will see your expertise!

Here are some examples of what measurable results looks like in a resume:

Sales/Marketing Example
Vice President, Marketing, TJ Kelly Electrical Contractors, Inc., Sussex, NJ, April 2002 to Present

- Oversee all direct sales and marketing efforts of this small, privately owned, independent electrical subcontractor that provides services to owners/developers, general contractors, and construction management companies.

- Generate approximately two invitations to bid weekly from account base by playing key role in bid package presentations, owner and/or owner rep meetings.

- Developed business plan to penetrate local, regional and national private construction sector via direct sales, qualified firm with 220+ accounts with project management and estimating teams for whom company is now capable of receiving bid requests.

- Developed prospecting source for business, yielding future potential pipeline of 140+ jobs.

- Directed cost-effective development of web site that provides information on firm's credentials, references, and capabilities, and can receive RFIs and RFPs directly from contractors and owners/developers.

- Coordinated installation of ISDN phone lines and Auto Cad to support web based initiatives.

- Led sales increase of $2+ million from 2001 to 2002, as well as sales that are currently trending higher in 2003 vs. 2002, with expected 2003 sales of $10 million.

IT Example
Project Manager, BJD Trading, New York, NY, 1989 to 1994

- Decreased annual operating budget by $2M, enhanced productivity, and saved customers $3.2M.
- Saved $1M in annual processing/communication fees by developing new system.
- Delivered consistent success in planning, development, and leadership of IT and operational projects, programs, resources, prioritizations, risk analyses, technologies, and process innovations that established industry precedents and contributed to productivity, efficiency, and bottom-line performance.
- Administered operating, capital, and project budgets of up to $7M.
- Managed up to 10 direct reports and up to 25 personnel.
- Regularly presented program/project plans to board of directors.
- Successfully managed post-integration issues through all mergers including the transition from Chicago Stock Exchange subsidiary to Federal Security Clearing Corp subsidiary with 800+ employees in 1995, to an FSCC affiliate with 100+ employees in 2001, and to current Investor Trust Company subsidiary with 3,000+ employees in 2002.

Manufacturing Supervisor Sample
Shift Supervisor, Norton Corporation, Santa Fe, NM, 1992 to 1997

- Sales Growth Contribution: Played key role in increasing sales from $1.2M to $5.1M in a 3 year time frame through effective marketing, sales and operations management strategies. Provided customer service to clients during on-site customer visits.

- Performance Improvement: Directed a team of ten employees in the manufacturing of professional medical equipment.

- Operations Reengineering: Streamlined packaging and shipping process, resulting in an annual savings of $500K.

Machinist Example

Machinist, CNC and Manual, Iverson Industries, Wyandotte, MI, 10/1994 to 08/2008 (company went out of business)

- Performed conversational programming on CNC lathe, Dynapath, including some G codes.

- Experienced with Fanuc G codes.

- Operated multiple lathes, both CNC & manual.

- Operated both large and small manual Nardini Lathes.

- Operated several of the machines that were included in the purchase of the business from Dodge & Dodge/Anlock Machine Products.

- Converted the plant from manual machinery to CNC machinery. Retrofitted older machines with the new CNC technology.

- Processed and quoted various jobs.

- Operated a CNC Lathe with Dynapath (retrofitted).

- Operated Gisholt turret lathe, 30" swing.

- Operated a manual Monarch 50".

- Operated Warner/Swayze, 30" swing Cellars Boring Mill 5" spindle.

- Operated GNL Boring Mill 3" spindle.

- Operated a Nardini Lathe, 42" swing, Bridgeport, Boring Mill 4" spindle called Shebura.

- Operated Okuma Howe 36", done with G codes, Fanuc control Bridgeport standard (several outdated unusable mills) and American maximum 27" swing and 92" long.

BE CLEAR AND SPECIFIC

Be sure to give extremely specific descriptions of your skillsets. One of the biggest pet peeves hiring managers have, as they are reading and reviewing resumes, is the lack of defined skillsets of the job seeker. To say that you "have knowledge of how to use a computer" without telling the types and versions of that software is of absolutely no value to the person reviewing your resume. If you can use Microsoft Word, Excel, PowerPoint, etc., it should be spelled out on your resume. Remember, BE SPECIFIC!

Because of the volume of resumes potential employers receive, it would be almost impossible for them to carefully read each and every one. Recruiters and potential employers, are trained to look for specific keywords. If you don't have the right keywords in your resume, you'll never make it past the first review.

Don't force them to guess how skilled or talented you are. If you leave them guessing, most likely your resume will be bypassed. Most employers don't care or have time to figure it out. If you do not show your skills and talents on your resume, managers will assume you don't have them.

THE COVER LETTER

A cover letter is like a cover on a book. We have all heard the expression, "Don't judge a book by its cover," but the truth is, if a book cover doesn't catch your eye, you'll probably walk right by it.

A solid cover letter should be written differently for each job or company to which you apply. The specific details of the cover letter will depend on your level of job experience and the type of job for which you are looking. The cover letter from a 20-year business executive, for example, is going to be quite different from the cover letter of a recently graduated college student.

Following, are some examples of different levels of cover letters. Choose one that you are comfortable with and add in your own words and experiences. Remember to BRAG! It's all about you!

Recent College Graduate Cover Letter

This cover letter is from a recently graduated collegiate, seeking her first job. She talks about her academic skillset, since she doesn't have relevant job accomplishments to discuss. The graduate usually looks to sell his or her soft skills (personality and characteristics) to the employer, with the hope of developing hard skills (job accomplishments and relevant work experience) further down the line.

Jane Doe
123 Street, Workersville, MI 48207
Cell 555-555-4567
jane.doe@email.com

Mr./Ms. Hiring Manager
Great Company Inc.
456 Street, Workersville, MI 48207

October 20, 2015

Dear Mr./Ms. Hiring Manager,

I am applying for the Inside Sales position posted on Monster.com. At your convenience, I'd appreciate the opportunity to discuss the position and my candidacy with you. I am looking to successfully bring my well-honed online, verbal, and interpersonal public relations, marketing, and client-focused skills to an inside sales position with Great Company, Inc. Please find my resume attached to this e-mail.

Pertinent experience and skills for the posted position include the following:

The power of persuasion. I have pitched stories for C-level executives via phone and e-mail and placed them in major media outlets, such as MSNBC, CIO Magazine, Sirius Satellite Radio, MSN Money, AARP Bulletin, and The New York Daily News.

The ability to reach key audiences. As a journalist, I have published stories in key print and online media, including CareerJournal.com, CollegeJournal.com and StartupJournal.com (online publications of The Wall Street Journal), Consumers Digest, Woman's Day, and ePregnancy Magazine. As a copywriter, my work has been used in email marketing, online and offline advertising, blogs, brochures, taglines, and web sites.

Strong financial aptitude: My experience includes a little over a decade in the accounting profession in external and internal client-facing environments.

B.S. in Accounting from Southern New Hampshire University, with a Minor in Management Information Systems.

Relevant computer skills: Microsoft products, HTML, etc.

I would love to find out more about the position you're looking to fill, and I would welcome the opportunity to tell you how my skills and ideas can benefit Great Company. I can be reached at (555) 555-4567 or jane.doe@email.com.

Thanks for your consideration; I look forward to hearing from you soon!

Sincerely,

Your Signature Here

Your Typed Name

Experienced/Changing Industries Cover Letter

A cover letter for someone looking to change careers should focus on transferable skills, along with an awareness that they will need to, and are willing to learn new skills and information. This person is changing from a job as a restaurant manager and is looking to move into a job in the recruiting field.

Mr. John Doe
456 Job Search Way
Workersville, MI 48207
555-555-6789
john.doe@email.com

Mr./Ms. Hiring Manager
Great Company Inc.
1234 Main Street
Anytown, MI 48124

June 20, 2015

Dear Mr./Ms. Hiring Manager,

Today I saw your post on Monster.com and was pleased to find that you are hiring for a recruiter. I am hoping to make a career change—from restaurant manager to recruiter.

It may sound like a stretch, but I see it as a real possibility and that is why I am writing this cover letter. I have spent the last ten years working with customers, handing complaints, upselling and dealing with staffing issues. Now that I am more experienced I want to bring my skills and begin helping other companies locate the staff they need.

I hope you will consider speaking to me about how I can fill this opening at your firm. Please phone me at 555-555-6789 if you'd like me to come in for an interview.

I appreciate this chance to introduce myself and to tell you about my plans to make this career change. Thank you for your time.

Thanks for your consideration; I look forward to hearing from you soon!

Sincerely,

Your Signature Here

Your Typed Name

USE SPELL CHECK!

You would be surprised at how many employers turn down perfect candidates simply because words are misspelled on their resumes. Misspelled words indicate carelessness and laziness and labels the job seeker as someone who lacks attention to detail. Don't let spelling errors come between you and a great job opportunity!

Spell checking tips:

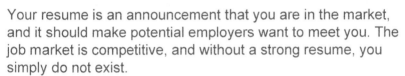

- **Use it!**
- **If you list a type or brand of machine or software you used, make sure you know exactly how it is spelled.**
- **After spell check is complete, print out your documents and read them. You'll catch things printed that you didn't see on your computer screen.**
- **Ask a friend/family member to read over your documents, and have them point out anything that they don't understand. This will help you to clarify things a recruiter or hiring manager may find unclear.**

Your resume is an announcement that you are in the market, and it should make potential employers want to meet you. The job market is competitive, and without a strong resume, you simply do not exist.

The format and wording of your resume are crucial to moving into the next phase of The Job Search Process™. It is vital that you know your resume inside and out. Take great pride in what it says. When it comes down to it, your resume is YOU on paper! Be proud, but also ask yourself, "Would I hire me?"

Once you know the type of job you seek, and are backed with a great resume, you can begin the process of getting yourself in front of potential future employers. Success requires sending out 100 resumes per week, every week, until you have a job. Broadcast your message loudly and frequently. You are the only spokesperson you have.

And now, the search is on!

LOCATE AND APPLY FOR JOB OPPORTUNITIES

Welcome to your new career…finding a job. The good news is that finding a job is a temporary position that will last six weeks or less, depending on how good you are at it. Commit to spending 40 hours a week looking for a job. Your strong commitment is what will keep you on track.

Below is a sample of a job seeker's full-time work week. Consider setting up a similar schedule for yourself to help avoid getting burned out. Be sure to hold yourself accountable for keeping it. Let's take a look and see how the week looks. (Hey! You get weekends off!)

WEEKLY SCHEDULE

Personal Time   Job Search   Social Media   Phone Calls   Resume/Cover Letter   Research   Exercise   **Reading**   Shopping   Interviews

	MONDAY	TUESDAY	WEDNESDAY	THURSDAY	FRIDAY
6:00 AM	Wake up/prep for the day				
7:00					
8:00	Search for jobs and post resumes	Mail out 20 resumes and cover letters	Schedule interviews here	Mail out 20 resumes and cover letters	Read "Awaken the Giant Within"
9:00					
10:00					Follow up calls
11:00	Social media		Social media		
12:00 PM	LUNCH				
1:00	Schedule interviews here	Shop for interview outfit	Follow up calls	Research companies I have interviews with and practice my 10 questions	Social media
2:00					Follow up calls
3:00			Search for jobs and post resumes		
4:00	Edit resume and cover letters	Search for jobs		Exercise at the gym	Search for jobs and post resumes
5:00		Yoga class			
6:00	Read		Read		
7:00					
8:00					

STAY POSITIVE

Setting up a structure for staying positive is critical. Start by making a declaration, first to yourself, and to others. If you are not currently employed, commit to spending 40 hours a week looking for a job. If you are employed or in school, get as close to 40 hours as time permits. Try something like, "I am going to spend 40 hours each and every week following The Job Search Process™ until I have a job that will take care of my family and me."

Write it down and post it EVERYWHERE! In your car. On your fridge. On the bathroom mirror. On the door leaving the house. On the bottom of the TV. On the computer screen. When it is always in front of you, it will serve as a constant reminder of your goals, to stay focused and press on!

TALK TO EVERYONE YOU MEET

Did you know that most people in the United States believe that every job opening is posted online, or is listed in their local newspaper?

The opposite is actually true. Only 15% of all jobs are ever listed, posted, or advertised.

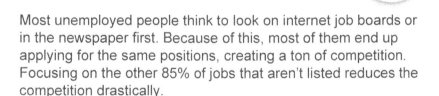

Most unemployed people think to look on internet job boards or in the newspaper first. Because of this, most of them end up applying for the same positions, creating a ton of competition. Focusing on the other 85% of jobs that aren't listed reduces the competition drastically.

The best way to get a job is through referrals, period. There is no quicker, more direct way to connect a person to their next job, than through someone who knows that the job opening exists. That is why you need to make a list of everyone you know – I mean everyone – and tell them you are looking for a job. From the mailman to your grandmother, don't leave anyone out. We are all interconnected. Take advantage of it!

Take a look at the list of best networking contacts below. Go through the exercise of listing everyone you know. (Grab your address book or your cell phone to help you with this.) See how many people you can list! Go ahead. Give it a try!

For college students and new grads:

- Classmates
- Alumni, especially recent grads
- Parents
- Parents of friends/classmates
- Other relatives
- Professors, especially your advisor
- Fraternity brothers, sorority sisters, and Greek organization alumni
- College administrators
- Coaches
- Guest speakers in your classes
- Informational interviewees

For established job seekers:

- Members of professional organizations
- Your past or present co-workers
- Friends you're in touch with regularly
- Old friends, like college buddies, whom you see infrequently
- Members of your religious community
- Peer volunteers
- Informational interviewees
- Your kids' friends' parents
- Your mentor(s)
- Business associates, customers, clients, vendors, and suppliers

Tell every single person who comes near you that you are in the job market. Ask if they know anyone who can help you. Hand out a condensed resume, on a business card, with your contact info on it to every person you meet. You never know who they might know and pass your information on to! This "networking business card" will make it very easy to pass along your information to employers who could be looking for someone with precisely your skills and talents. Be sure to list specific skills you have and that you are looking for work.

NETWORKING BUSINESS CARD SAMPLE

James A. Carter

Career Goal: Chartered Accountant

 Resume/Profile Link *(Monster, LinkedIn, Twitter, etc.)*

* 3rd year UTM Bachelor of Commerce student
* Accounting/Finance & Economics specialist
* Working toward completion of IACO

jacareer@utoronto.ca

You can design your own! This card was created at www.vistaprint.com with one of their easy-to-use templates. As low as $16 for a box of 100 *(plus shipping)*.

Just remember to keep it clean and simple like the example above.

INTERNET…
WHAT'S THAT?

Some job seekers aren't very familiar with the internet, or don't have consistent internet access. If this is the case, you can still get much of the same contact information for companies you might like to work for with paper resources. Consider trying your public library, the yellow pages, and your local newspaper.

Your public library will have everything you need to conduct a successful job search. They will have business and industry directories, and local and regional phone books. In addition, most libraries have computers with an internet connection, in case you choose to turn to internet research. Many state agencies also provide resources to job seekers, free of charge.

 Getting to know:
LINKEDIN
www.linkedin.com

LinkedIn is quickly becoming the favorite tool of recruiters and employers worldwide to locate job seekers for their openings. The site operates on the theory that anyone you need or want to meet is less than six degrees away from you. That means someone you know probably knows someone who knows the person you'd like to contact. LinkedIn provides an easy way for you to contact that person and have your message passed through the network until it gets to the person you're trying to reach.

LinkedIn works best when you're connected to people you actually know, because those are the people most likely to pass along your message. LinkedIn is like an engine for networking leads and introductions.

Other things you can do on LinkedIn include:

- Building an extensive resume of your work

- Adding a status update that is seen in the news feeds of all of your contacts

- Integrating your blog feed, Slideshare presentations or a number of new applications, including Tripit to show your business travel

- Asking and answering questions from the larger LinkedIn community

- Setting up or joining LinkedIn groups for like-minded discussions

- Asking for recommendations or recommending someone you've worked with in the past

 Getting to know:
FACEBOOK
www.facebook.com

Facebook was created as more of a social, rather than business network. Because of this, its use as a professional networking tool is still relatively new and undergoing transitions as the company continues to update their interface and change their policies.

Some things you can do with your Facebook account that can be useful for business include:

- Reconnecting with old high school and college contacts for potential business networking

- Creating a Facebook Page to build a fan base that can receive strategic marketing announcements from you

- Starting a Facebook Group for discussions

- Adding Facebook Events to the Facebook searchable calendar to expand your event's exposure

- Recruiting people to support important issues through the Causes application

- Integrating your social media with applications for Twitter, Friendfeed, blog feeds and more…

Both LinkedIn and Facebook provide tools on their web sites to help you get started on setting up accounts. If you prefer to have a video tutorial on how to set your accounts up, there are several videos on YouTube (www.youtube.com) that walk you through the steps of setting up and using these tools.

Beyond making yourself known to recruiters, social media is a quick and effective method for letting people in your extended network know that you are in the job market.

POST YOUR RESUME ON ALL JOB BOARDS

How can employers find you if they don't know you exist?

There are several major job boards, www.monster.com, www.indeed.com, www.ziprecruiter.com, www.simplyhired.com and www.careerbuilder.com, where you should post your resume.

Also take a look at what job boards your state offers for specific areas. For example, Michigan has the Michigan Talent Bank, where all unemployed people in the state are required to post their resumes, in order to receive unemployment benefits.

Hiring managers, recruiters and HR professionals also look at niche job boards that are specific to certain industries or skillsets. There are also freelance job boards that allow you to work on short-term projects, such as www.guru.com. On the following pages is a list of job boards separated by niche — check it out and then get posting!

You should also check out www.yellowpages.com and www.superpages.com. On those sites, typing in keywords, a location, and a travel distance, produces a list of all the companies in your that area that contain your keyword. For example, on Superpages, a medical assistant looking for work in pediatrics typed in the keyword "pediatrics," along with her ideal city, and the distance she was willing to travel. A total of 496 results were displayed. She sent her resume to the first 200, and got six interviews and six job offers! Remember, none of those jobs were posted on a job board or advertised in any newspaper.

Another highly successful method is to conduct an internet search based on your past employers, or on employers for which you would like to work. Using Google, Yahoo, Bing or another search engine, type in the company name and some keywords pertaining to the business and the search engine will create a list of the original company's competitors.

NICHE JOB BOARD
(courtesy of Eric Shannon at LatPro, Inc.)

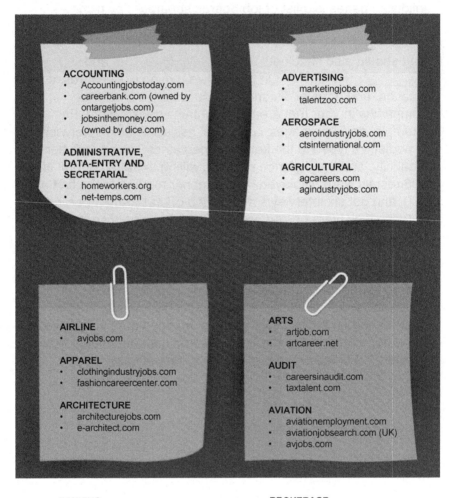

ACCOUNTING
- Accountingjobstoday.com
- careerbank.com (owned by ontargetjobs.com)
- jobsinthemoney.com (owned by dice.com)

ADMINISTRATIVE, DATA-ENTRY AND SECRETARIAL
- homeworkers.org
- net-temps.com

ADVERTISING
- marketingjobs.com
- talentzoo.com

AEROSPACE
- aeroindustryjobs.com
- ctsinternational.com

AGRICULTURAL
- agcareers.com
- agindustryjobs.com

AIRLINE
- avjobs.com

APPAREL
- clothingindustryjobs.com
- fashioncareercenter.com

ARCHITECTURE
- architecturejobs.com
- e-architect.com

ARTS
- artjob.com
- artcareer.net

AUDIT
- careersinaudit.com
- taxtalent.com

AVIATION
- aviationemployment.com
- aviationjobsearch.com (UK)
- avjobs.com

BANKING
- bankjobs.com
- careerbank.com (owned by ontargetjobs.com)

BIOTECH
- biohealthmatics.com
- biospace.com
- medzilla.com

BROADCAST
- amfmjobs.com
- careerpage.org
- tvjobs.com

BROKERAGE
- brokerhunter.com

CALL CENTER
- callcentercareers.com
- callcenterclassifieds.com
- callcenterjobs.com

CHILDCARE
- care.com
- greataupair.com
- nannies4hire.com

COMMUNICATIONS
- writejobs.com

NICHE JOB BOARD
(part two)

COMPUTERS & SYTEMS
- computerjobs.com (owned by JobServe.com)
- computerwork.com (owned by JobServe.com)
- dice.com
- gjc.com
- tech-centric.net

CONSTRUCTION
- constructionexecutive.com
- constructionjobs.com
- mepjobs.com
- topbuildingjobs.com

CREATIVE
- krop.com
- creativejobscentral.com

CUSTOMER SERVICE
- callcentercareers.com
- employmentguide.com (owned by Landmark Communications)

DATABASE
- databasejobs.com
- dbjobs.org

DEFENSE
- defense.com

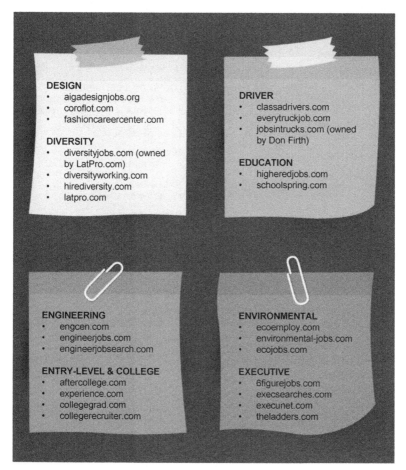

DESIGN
- aigadesignjobs.org
- coroflot.com
- fashioncareercenter.com

DIVERSITY
- diversityjobs.com (owned by LatPro.com)
- diversityworking.com
- hirediversity.com
- latpro.com

DRIVER
- classadrivers.com
- everytruckjob.com
- jobsintrucks.com (owned by Don Firth)

EDUCATION
- higheredjobs.com
- schoolspring.com

ENGINEERING
- engcen.com
- engineerjobs.com
- engineerjobsearch.com

ENTRY-LEVEL & COLLEGE
- aftercollege.com
- experience.com
- collegegrad.com
- collegerecruiter.com

ENVIRONMENTAL
- ecoemploy.com
- environmental-jobs.com
- ecojobs.com

EXECUTIVE
- 6figurejobs.com
- execsearches.com
- execunet.com
- theladders.com

NICHE JOB BOARD
(part three)

FASHION
- stylecareers.com
- fashioncareercenter.com
- clothingindustryjobs.com

FINANCE & INVESTMENT
- careerbank.com (owned by ontargetjobs.com)
- jobsinthemoney.com (owned by dice.com)
- efinancialcareers.com (owned by dice.com)

FITNESS & WELLNESS
- fitnessjobs.com
- exercisecareers.com
- exercisejobs.com

FOOD SERVICE
- foodindustryjobs.com
- foodservice.com

FORESTRY
- treecarejobs.com

GOVERNMENT
- usajobs.gov
- governmentjobs.com
- govtjobs.com

HEALTHCARE & MEDICAL
- healthcareerweb.com
- healthecareers.com owned by ontargetjobs.com
- healthjobsusa.com
- medhunters.com
- medicalworkers.com

HOME
- worldwideworkathome.com
- jobsformoms.com
- tjobs.com

HOSPITALITY & HOTEL
- hcareers.com
- hospitalityonline.com
- hoteljobs.com

HOURLY
- snagajob.com
- employmentguide.com
- groovejob.com

HR
- jobs4hr.com
- jobs.shrm.org
- workforcehrjobs.com

INSURANCE
- greatinsurancejobs.com
- insurancejobs.com
- ultimateinsurancejobs.com

INTERNATIONAL
- internationaljobs.org
- intljobs.org

INTERNSHIP
- internjobs.com
- aftercollege.com
- campuscareercenter.com

JOURNALISM
- journalismjobs.com
- newsjobs.com

LABORATORY & TECHNICIAN
- healthjobsusa.com

LAW ENFORCEMENT
- 911hotjobs.com
- lawenforcementjobs.com
- policeemployment.com

LAW
- attorneyjobs.com
- emplawyernet.com
- lawjobs.com

LOGISTICS & DISTRIBUTION
- jobsinlogistics.com (owned by Don Firth)
- jobsinmanufacturing.com (owned by Don Firth)
- maritimejobs.com

MAINTENANCE
- hvacagent.com

MACHINING
- getmachinistjobs.com

MANUFACTURING
- jobsinmanufacturing.com (owned by Don Firth)
- manufacturingjobs.com

MARKETING
- marketingjobs.com
- talentzoo.com

MEDIA
- massmediajobs.com
- mediabistro.com (owned by JupiterMedia.com)
- varietycareers.com (owned by ReedBusiness.com)

MINING
- miningjobs.org
- minejob.com
- miscojobs.com

NEWS
- newsjobs.com

NICHE JOB BOARD
(part four)

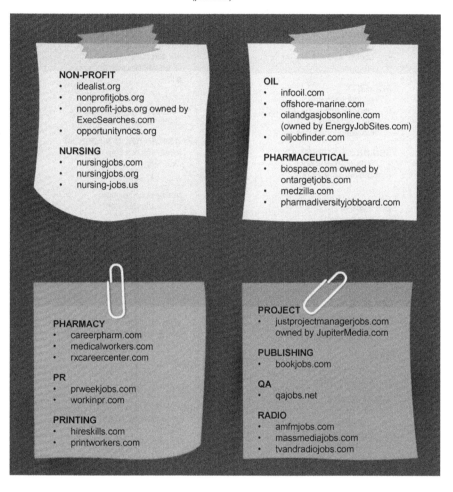

NON-PROFIT
- idealist.org
- nonprofitjobs.org
- nonprofit-jobs.org owned by ExecSearches.com
- opportunitynocs.org

NURSING
- nursingjobs.com
- nursingjobs.org
- nursing-jobs.us

OIL
- infooil.com
- offshore-marine.com
- oilandgasjobsonline.com (owned by EnergyJobSites.com)
- oiljobfinder.com

PHARMACEUTICAL
- biospace.com owned by ontargetjobs.com
- medzilla.com
- pharmadiversityjobboard.com

PHARMACY
- careerpharm.com
- medicalworkers.com
- rxcareercenter.com

PR
- prweekjobs.com
- workinpr.com

PRINTING
- hireskills.com
- printworkers.com

PROJECT
- justprojectmanagerjobs.com owned by JupiterMedia.com

PUBLISHING
- bookjobs.com

QA
- qajobs.net

RADIO
- amfmjobs.com
- massmediajobs.com
- tvandradiojobs.com

REAL ESTATE
- real-jobs.com
- selectleaders.com

RECRUITING
- ere.net

RESTAURANT
- hcareers.com
- starchefsjobfinder.com

RETAIL
- allretailjobs.com (owned by Don Firth)
- fashioncareercenter.com

SAFETY
- ehscareers.com
- environmentaljobs.com

SALES
- marketingjobs.com
- salesjobs.com
- salestrax.com

SCIENCE
- nature.com (magazine/journal)
- sciencejobs.org
- scjobs.sciencemag.org

NICHE JOB BOARD
(part five)

SEASONAL
- backdoorjobs.com
- coolworks.com
- jobmonkey.com

SECURITY
- securityjobs.net
- clearancejobs.com {owned by Dice.com)
- clearedconnections.com

SENIOR & RETIREMENT
- retirementjobs.com
- seniorjobbank.org

SOFTWARE
- prgjobs.com

SPORTS
- jobsinsports.com
- sportscareerfinder.com
- teamworkonline.com
- workinsports.com

SUPPLY
- jobsinlogistics.com (owned by Don Firth)
- supplychainjobs.com

TAX
- careersintax.com
- taxtalent.com

TECHNOLOGY
- dice.com
- justtechjobs.com (owned by JupiterMedia.com)
- tech-centric.net

TELECOM & WIRELESS
- tech-centric.net
- telecomcareers.net
- wirelessjobs.com (community site)

THERAPY
- therapyjobs.com (owned by HealthcareJobBoards.com)

TRANSPORTATION & AIRPORT
- jobsinlogistics.com (owned by Don Firth)

TV
- massmediajobs.com
- tvandradiojobs.com
- tvjobs.com

UNDERWRITING
- insuranceunderwritingweb.com
- IAEWS (owned by Insurance Jobs.com)
- underwritingjobs.com

UTILITY
- energyjobsearch.com
- utilityjobsonline.com
- utility-worker.com (owned by EnergyJobSites.com)

VETERAN
- militaryjobzone.com
- vetjobs.com

VOLUNTEER
- backdoorjobs.com
- idealist.org
- volunteermatch.org

WAREHOUSE
- warehousejobs.com

TRACK YOUR JOB SEARCH

How many jobs did you apply for this week?
What key phrases have you used in your searches?
Which ones produced the best jobs?
A potential employer calls you for an on the spot phone
interview…can you quickly look through your notes and
find the resume and cover letter used?

When I was a job seeker, I found it helpful to set up a system to manage my contact information and correspondence with prospective employers. For example, I would send out the resumes on Monday, and call to follow up that Friday. This showed a sense of urgency and interest on my part, as well as my ability to follow through.

Using Excel or a paper notebook, write down all of the names, addresses, telephone numbers, and dates you make contact, for every company to which you send your resume. Also note where you found the position. Most employers are interested to know that.

Staying organized in the Job Search Process™ is a key component to success. It is vital to keep accurate records to avoid frustration and embarrassment. For example, if you receive a return call on a resume you sent out and the potential employer wants to do a telephone interview on the spot, it is very helpful to have all of your notes at your fingertips to demonstrate your credibility and organization to the interviewer.

If the company is worth sending a resume to then they are worth making a follow-up call. Believe it or not, some companies will wait to hear from you before they contact you. This is intentional. They want to see how aggressive you are and how badly you want that job!

FOLLOW UP. BE PERSISTENT.

It can be extremely difficult to reach potential employers on the telephone. These people are often busy doing several different tasks, and hiring is just one of them. By being pleasantly persistent with your follow-up call, you are leaving a positive first impression.

Remember, it is your job to give them a reason to call you back. If you have to leave a voicemail, be very pleasant, and have high energy in your voice. State clearly what you feel you will bring to the company, in a short, concise manner. Let them know that you will call back in a few days if you have not heard back from them.

SAMPLE TRACKING SHEET

Company Name	Contact Information	Contact Name	Notes	Resume Sent	Follow-up Date	Follow-up Date	Follow-up Date	Interview Date
Ford Motor Company	800-123-4567 123 Ford Road Detroit, MI 41234	Henry Ford	Applied for IT Intern position	1/2/2009	1/7/2009			
Detroit Distributors	313-456-7890 999 Telegraph Detroit, MI 12345	Mary Smith	Spoke to HR on 1/3, told to call back on 1/6	12/28/2008	1/3/2009	1/6/2009		
Michigan Manufacturers	248-123-4567 4567 Woodward Detroit, MI 48484	Joseph Job	Application deadline is 2/2	1/29/2009	2/4/2009			

For example:

"Hello, Mr./Ms. _____, this is Bob Smith. I sent you my resume two days ago and I wanted to talk with you more about why I feel I would be a good addition to the team at _____. With my more than 10 years of experience in your industry at _____, I feel I could be a productive team member from day one of my employment with _____. Please call me back at _____. If I don't hear back from you soon, I will call you back in two days. Thank you! Goodbye."

ASK FOR THE HIRING MANAGER, SETTLE FOR HR

Hiring managers, regardless of the industry, often have to get more work done with less talent every day. They have deadlines, customer issues, and budgetary challenges. This creates a great many headaches for them, and this "pain" is very likely where someone with your skills and talents can help. The only way you can help, however, is to actually talk to that person.

Much of the time, when a resume comes to a company, it is sent to the human resources (HR) department. Since the HR department and hiring manager aren't always on the same page when it comes to upcoming job openings, the HR department is often where resumes go to die.

If the hiring manager is planning to get rid of an under-performing employee, HR may or may not be aware that change is going to take place. In many organizations the hiring manager is the final decision maker concerning who ends up getting hired, not HR. Don't go to the middle man. Go to the final decision maker whenever possible.

MAKE THEM WANT TO MEET YOU

By having a solid resume, asking good questions, following through, and having an engaging demeanor on the telephone, you are creating reasons why the hiring manager would want to meet with you.

If all else fails, invite your connection/potential employer to lunch. Everyone likes a free meal! Lunch is a great environment for you to discuss the potential of working for the company. Lunch usually has a beginning and ending time, is casual and less stressful on everyone involved, including you. This will also set you apart from your job competitors, demonstrating your creativity and uniqueness. I can guarantee you that no one else competing for the same position will have invited the potential employer to lunch (unless they have taken my course)!

Here is a good way to ask:

"Mr./Ms. Hiring Manager, I know that you probably have a great number of candidates for this position. I am so interested in your company, I would welcome the chance for us to get together for lunch, so that we can discuss what you are looking for in your ideal hire. Please allow me the opportunity to buy you lunch. Is Tuesday or Thursday this week better for you?"

IT NEVER HURTS TO ASK

If you want something badly enough, you need ask for it. If you have the key decision maker on the phone, don't let him/her off the phone without asking for an in-person interview. I have often found that the persistent candidate is the one who gets the interview.

CONGRATULATIONS ON YOUR FIRST INTERVIEW!

Sigh with relief, you're there!

Next up: The interview.
Interviewing can be one of the most nerve wracking experiences of your professional life. Some people walk into interviews unprepared, hoping to get by on conversation skills alone. That is a formula for disaster.

Treat each job interview as a final exam. Prepare ahead of time by studying facts about the company and about the position. This preparation will provide you with a sense of calm and confidence. It will also give you a leg up on your competitors.

Every interview gets you one step closer to landing yourself a job, so make every single one worthwhile. Study company facts, practice sample answers, and get a full night's sleep so that you can walk in refreshed, confident, and ready to dazzle your interviewers. Make them want to hire you.

CONDUCT INTERNET RESEARCH

The internet is the by far the most valuable tool that you can use to be able to successfully complete the Job Search Process™. You will able to learn a massive amount of information about the company you are interviewing with, including the following:

- Their industry
- What the company specifically does

- Who their competitors are
- Who their customers are
- Any media exposure they have had
- The names of the staff or management team
- Other job openings they have
- Expansion or contraction plans they have

Look up the web site of the company you are interviewing with. You will want to create a fact sheet on the company to take with you to the interview. This will be a quick-reference "cheat sheet" that you can use if you get nervous during the interview.

BACKGROUND-CHECK YOUR INTERVIEWER

On top of knowing the facts about the company, you need to make sure you know who you will be conducting your interview. For example, are you meeting with the president and CEO? The plant manager? The human resources manager? The foreman? A peer from your potential future department?

Studies have shown that everyone's favorite word is their own name. The person interviewing you will be immensely impressed, and even flattered, that you took the time to learn about him or her. Look for information about the person's position within the company, amount of time with the company, and any hobbies or fun facts about them. Any information you gather could help you bond with your interviewer. Just be sure to steer clear of personal topics like family, children, or religious preferences.

How will you find this information? I suggest you visit the company website, conduct a Google search on the person's name, and investigate which social networks they belong to, such as LinkedIn, and Facebook.

INTERVIEW PREP 4

PREPARE:
DO NOT WING IT

It's an interview. They are going to ask you questions that you probably aren't asked every day. There are many guides floating around out there regarding how to interview in today's society. Chances are the person interviewing you will have read one or more of these. You should read a few as well. This information will help you prepare your answers ahead of time, instead of feeling caught off guard or put on the spot.

The ultimate interview question an interviewer can ask is, "I have 5 qualified candidates, one of which is you. Why should I hire *you*?" Should they ask you this question, you need to be able to know your answer like the back of your hand. State it clearly and confidently, because your competition may or may not know theirs.

Knowing what you may be asked can help you prepare for any trick questions. You'll have solid answers ready to go at the drop of a hat. This will not only impress the interviewer, but will also help you stand out from your competition.

For example, interviewers will often ask you about your weaknesses. They are not looking for you to say that you are often late for work or that you cannot get along with your co-workers! A solid answer to this question would be: "I am often very hard on myself and take my work seriously. I sometimes skip my lunch to finish a project or assignment and end up eating unhealthily. So in order to overcome that, I will often bring my lunch and eat at my desk."

Behavioral Interviewing:

Behavioral interview questions are very popular in today's marketplace. They are designed to get you, the interviewee, to share examples of how you have reacted to or handled situations in the past. By knowing your answers to behavioral questions in advance, you will be prepared and comfortable telling some tremendous stories showing what a great employee you are.

For example, a behavioral question might be:

"Give me an example of a time when you showed initiative and took the lead." A strong answer to that would be, *"At my last job, when layoffs and downsizing were going on, I offered to take on new duties and responsibilities that I knew would cause me to have to come in early and stay late each day. I did it because I knew it was what the company needed to have happen and I am proud to say that by taking on those extra responsibilities when times were tough, I was acknowledged by my superiors with a promotion to department manager."*

Because you never know what type of behavioral questions will be asked, I suggest that you have a simple answer prepared for each example below. This might take some time and thought, but I know once you answer these questions you will feel very confident about your next behavioral interview.

Let's take a look.

Sample Company Cheat Sheet

Company Name:
Woodland Direct, Inc.

What they do:
Online retail sales of fireplace, chimney, and 'everything outdoors'. Strictly online sales, worldwide.

Competitors:
American Fireplace, Canada's Chimneys

Customers:
Contractors, distributors, large home owners, clients who make $125K or more, annually.

Media exposure:
Extreme Home Makeover donation

Staff/Management:
Andrew Seller and Marcus Market

Other job openings:
Accounting, HR Manager

Expansion plans:
Add 3 new companies and over 250 new products by 2020.

Some of the most frequently asked interview questions, with suggested response types:

Why do you want to work here?
Have your company/organization "cheat sheet" completed and ready. Give just one or two reasons why you are interested, like the company's reputation or the desire to join a specific field of interest.

Where do you want to be in 5 years?
Do not appear to be overly ambitious or speak in a way that implies you would not be satisfied with the job for which you have you have applied. Say something like, "I would like to be frank. Judge me by my work, and I am sure you will put me right where I want to be."

Why are you leaving your current job?
You should give two or three reasons for leaving, such as lack of challenge. Focus on the limitations. Confidently point out your ambition to prove your worth.

Why should we hire you?
This is often the concluding question in an interview scenario. Do not repeat your resume and do not list your experiences. Instead, prove your interest in the job and the organization. Make sure your answer demonstrates how you can be a solution to the needs of the hiring manager.

How do you manage your work to meet deadlines?
Answer the question effectively. Describe, in detail, how you plan out your time each day, setting priorities, determining schedules, following up, checking on progress and meeting the dead line.

How do you handle criticism?
The interviewer will use this question to determine your

accountability and professional character. Simply explain a situation that caused a problem and narrate how you faced it and overcame it.

Tell me about a situation that upset you at work.
Here the interview is trying to find out how you deal with pressure. Be diplomatic and objective with your answer. Prepare the answer so that the answer comes as a smooth reassurance.

KNOW WHO IS THE ULTIMATE DECISION MAKER

Many companies have a multi-layered approach to hiring. This means, you may have to go through several interviews before getting an offer. They may have you meet with human resources, potential co-workers, even participate in a team interview. You cannot avoid this if it is their policy. There is, however, almost always one person who makes the ultimate decision of "yes" or "no". Your job is to find out who that person is. Though I call that person the "Hiring Manager," he or she may have a different job title depending upon the company with which you are interviewing.

Once you identify who the hiring manager is, either through research or by simply asking other people in the interview process, you will want to meet him or her before you leave the interview. Even if the interaction is brief, you will at least be able to try to read that person, in case they end up conducting a second interview with you.

It is always best to get an interview with the hiring manager, if possible. That's often the person you will be reporting to directly. If you can get connected with this person, discover what is important to them in a potential employee, and what they are missing in their current employees. This will help you customize your interview responses in a way that will be of benefit to them. That is incredibly important. You go from being just another candidate to being THE candidate, because you can help them do their job better, you can help heal whatever issues they face. You can help them get all of their work done in a timely manner and ultimately help the company as a whole.

PREPARE 10 COMPANY QUESTIONS

There is a very important unwritten rule out there: The interviewer expects you to have questions about the position.

Most interviewers will conclude your interview by asking you if you have any questions for them, and even if they don't ask, it is your responsibility to inform them that you have a few questions about the company and the job opening.

Don't feel that you need to wait until the end of the interview to ask questions though. Sprinkle them, if possible, throughout the interview to avoid interrogating the interviewer at the end of your interview.

It is important to have your questions prepared and written down prior to going to your interview. This will allow you to stay on task with your questioning. You should ask questions to learn more about the company, its goals and objectives, why they are hiring, and what the company looks for in the people they hire. This is your chance to interview the company to see if they are good fit for you and your objectives.

Be sure to take notes on their answers so that you can refer back to them later. This is often helpful when you are involved in a multi-layered interview process. Sometimes individuals within the company can send mixed messages and your notes will allow you ask follow-up questions to the hiring manager or ultimate decision maker. Take a look at the sample questions below. This may help you create some questions on your own for your upcoming interview.

QUESTIONS TO ASK IN AN INTERVIEW
From Careerbuilder.com

The company:
- What do you see ahead for your company in the next five years?
- How do you see the future for this industry?
- What do you consider to be your firm's most important assets?
- What can you tell me about your new product or plans for growth?
- How do you rate your competition?

The position's history:
Asking about why the position is vacant can provide insight into the company and the potential for advancement.

Good questions include:
- What happened to the last person who held this job?
- What were his or her major strengths and weaknesses?
- What types of skills do you NOT already have on board that you're looking to fill with a new hire?

The department:
Asking about your department's workers and role in the company can help you understand more about the company's culture and hierarchy:

- What is the overall structure of the company and how does your department fit within that structure?
- What are the career paths in this department?
- What have been the department's successes in the last couple of years?
- How do you view your group/division/department?

The job's responsibilities:
To avoid any confusion later on, it pays to gain a solid understanding of the position.

- What would you consider to be the most important aspects of this job?
- What are the skills and attributes you value most for someone being hired for this position?
- Where have successful employees, who were previously in this position progressed to, within the company?
- Could you describe a typical day or week in this position? The typical client or customer I would be dealing with?

The expectations:
To determine how and when you will evaluated, ask:

- What are the most immediate challenges of the position that need to be addressed in the first three months?
- What are the performance expectations of this position over the first 12 months?
- How will I be evaluated at your company, and how often?

By taking time and preparing for the interview, you should be feeling self assured and confident. By committing to researching the company, and the interviewer, as well as studying potential interview questions, you are not leaving this portion of your Job Search Process™ to chance. You are preparing yourself for success. You are keeping the declaration you made to yourself, and your support system of family and friends.

Now is the time to put your preparation to the test in the interview arena!

ACE YOUR INTERVIEW 5

Be prepared and confident. There are 3 people for every 1 job in the USA (January, 2014), BE THE ONE THEY HIRE!

In strong or weak economic times there is one constant when it comes to interviewing for a job, you will have competition. Employers today will have many, many qualified applicants to choose from. This can be overwhelming for both the job seeker and for the companies. The job seeker, more often than not, needs the job. The employer, more often than not, needs to hire someone and feels overwhelmed with choices and options. The employer feels pressure to make the "perfect hire" or feels pressure to hire someone ASAP because they need to get work done. There is a swirl of emotions for everyone involved.

It is your job to make it easy for the company. Make yourself the best person for the job. Be the one they want to hire on the spot!

BE EARLY

If you're late, you'll give the impression that you are rude. Between a GPS, apps like Google Maps and Waze, and the old stand-by of getting directions from the receptionist, you have no excuse to be late for an interview. Arrive 15 minutes early. It shows the company that you are taking the interview seriously.

Plus, by arriving early, you'll have a chance to sit in the company's lobby. This can be very informative. Companies often have marketing information in the lobby, along with awards and media appearances, or pictures of key executives on their walls. This is your final chance to gather some competitive intelligence on the company.

When you arrive for the interview, be sure to introduce yourself to the receptionist. Tell her how excited you are to be interviewing with the company. If she is not too busy with her job responsibilities, talk to her as if she is the person with which you are interviewing. She may be able to give you some key insights about the job or the company. Also, many interviewers will ask the receptionist what their impression is of you. It doesn't hurt to have him or her on your side. Start making a positive impression as soon as you get there.

DRESS TO IMPRESS

It is very important to know the culture of the company at which you are interviewing. Part of that culture is the company dress code. Some dress codes are formal, and some are informal. In any case, it is always best to dress for a professional interview, even for a manual labor job. If you have a limited wardrobe, a good rule of thumb is to wear clothing that is appropriate for a wedding or a funeral. Here is a list of the proper interview attire for both women and men:

Women's Interview Attire:

- Solid color, conservative suit
- Coordinated blouse
- Moderate shoes
- Limited jewelry
- Neat, professional hairstyle

- Tan or light hosiery
- Sparse make-up & perfume
- Manicured nails
- Portfolio or briefcase

Men's Interview Attire:

- Solid color, conservative suit
- White long-sleeved shirt
- Conservative tie
- Dark socks, professional shoes
- Very limited jewelry
- Neat, professional hairstyle
- Go easy on the aftershave
- Neatly trimmed nails
- Portfolio or briefcase

"MIRROR" YOUR INTERVIEWER

Interviewers often base their hiring decisions on emotion, not logic. One of the best ways to connect with the interviewer, when you are face to face with them, is to use the mirroring technique. This simple, yet powerful bonding technique creates a signal to the other person that you are similar to them because you move like them. Pay attention to the interviewer and their non-verbal communication. If they sit very straight and lean forward, adopt a similar posture. If they sit back and slouch, you can relax and lean back a little, although you should maintain a professional appearance regardless of what the interviewer does. Mirroring can be extended to speaking style as well. If the interviewer speaks quickly, you should try to match their pace. Mirroring is a talent and a skill. Some people do it very naturally, while others struggle. To be most effective, you should mirror the interviewer almost unconsciously.

For example, I am an expressive talker when I am passionate about a topic — like finding a job. I use colorful adjectives, walk around while speaking, and make hand gestures to convey my message. If someone were to interview with me at my company, they would want to be very bubbly, high energy, and expressive in their verbal and non-verbal communication. By behaving that way, I would get the feeling that they were similar to me.

I am successful in my job and part of that success ties into who I am and how I communicate. In an interview, I would notice similar communication traits in the interviewee and more than likely I would like what I saw in them — because it is what I like about myself.

BE LIKEABLE

I often tell job candidates to treat a job interview like you would treat a first date. Always present yourself in the best way possible, while conveying a genuine sense of interest in the other person. Smile often and be authentic.

Perhaps the most quoted philosophy on smiling comes from Dale Carnegie's book *How To Win Friends and Influence People*. In it he writes, "It costs nothing, but creates much. It enriches those who receive, without impoverishing those who give. It happens in a flash and the memory of it sometimes lasts forever."

Other Positive Communication Techniques
(from Monster.com):

- Ensure a strong first impression through your handshake. Your handshake is key to making a good first impression.

- Use your eyes to communicate. Communicate enthusiasm, passion, importance, humor and interest in the employer. Think about making your eyes sparkle, it will go a long way in relaxing you and making your interview enjoyable.

- Keep your hair under control. There's nothing worse than watching a candidate fuss with his or her hair, or flip hair away from their face during a meeting. Hair fiddling is a sure sign of insecurity.

- Project confidence through your posture. Be sure your shoulders are square, your neck is straight, that you are holding your head high and your chest is open. Put your hands on your lap or your thighs, and be conscious not to cross your arms over your chest.

- Eliminate nervous fiddling. If you play with your rings and jewelry, don't wear any. The message here? Keep the interviewer's attention on you, not your fidgeting.

ASK TO TAKE NOTES

It is a very good idea to take notes during your interview but it is an even better idea to seek permission from the interviewer, before you take out your pen and paper. Always bring a note pad to your interview (along with five extra copies of your resume). Asking if the interviewer minds if you take notes lets them know that you are serious about the job. You are saying, indirectly, "What we are discussing is important to me. Important discussions get written down."

There is a tremendous amount of information exchanged at an interview. There is simply no way you can be expected to remember every detail. Don't pretend to have an incredible memory. If you don't take notes, it could make you appear uninterested and irresponsible. Especially when you ask a question that has already been explained.

BE HONEST

You might remember the case of George O'Leary, who was forced to resign five days after being hired as Notre Dame's head football coach because he lied on his resume about his educational degrees.

Studies show that 30% of all job seekers lie on their resume or during the interview process. There is no benefit to lying about skills, talents, abilities or degrees that you do not have. If you do get hired, the company expects you to be all that your resume says you are, and if they find out that it's not all true, you will get fired.

REMEMBER YOUR 10 QUESTIONS!

Interviewers expect you to have questions about the job and the company. By having a list prepared ahead of time, you won't forget to ask them. You can also add questions to you list while you are taking notes during the interview.

DON'T DISCUSS PAY OR BENEFITS AT THE FIRST INTERVIEW

It's a presumed fact that you, as the job seeker, are looking to be paid for the work that you will be doing for this company. Everyone in the room knows this. The time to discuss a compensation package (salary and benefits) is when the company offers you the job. Until then, it is not to be discussed. If you bring up how much you want to be paid, you could look selfish and ungrateful.

On the other hand, the interviewer may ask you how much money you are seeking in compensation. The best tactic is to change the subject. Simple statements such as "I don't want to box myself in, in terms of salary right now. If you don't mind, I'd like to focus on the value I can produce for your company," or "I'm sure we can come to a salary agreement, if I'm the right person for the job. I'd like to see if we agree that I am."

Often job seekers will blunder by jumping on the issue of compensation too soon and will sometimes price themselves out of job before they can show the value they would bring to the position.

FIND OUT WHAT'S NEXT

People are sometimes afraid to ask what the next step in the interview process is. They will simply wait to hear from the interviewer at some point in the future. This turns into a stressful waiting game which can be very frustrating. The only two words that matter are yes and no: "Yes, we want to offer you the job," or "No, we will not be offering you the job." Maybe doesn't get you anywhere.

Some next steps may include background and reference checks on you (have your references available when asked), a second interview with this person, a second interview with someone else (find out who, so you can do your research), interviews with other candidates, and then the final decision.

It is your responsibility to get a measureable timeline for the hiring process, to help you understand when you can expect to move forward with this company, and so that you know how to continue to schedule meetings with other potential employers.

Below is an example of one company's multi-layered hiring process. Keep in mind that some companies do just one interview and make their decision from there, and others have this type of interview process. Be prepared for either scenario. You can see why it may take quite some time for a company to make a final decision.

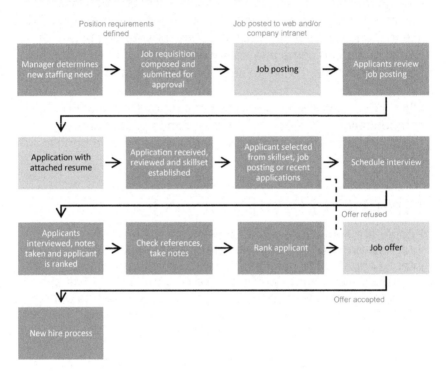

ASK FOR THE JOB

Even after they have told you what the next step will be, you're not done with the interview. Interviewers want to know that you are interested in working for their company. They are often disappointed when job seekers they interview do not ask for the job. While you are still face to face with them I suggest that you take the offensive route and ask for it.

These are two of my favorite approaches for doing this:

Summation Approach:
Lay out all the facts — the exact reasons there is a match between you and the employer. Here's an example:

"Throughout our conversation today, I have learned about the dynamics of your company, its culture, and the responsibilities of the position. I'm glad to see that your requirements match my experience to the letter — from my ability to manage corporate accounts to my ability to cultivate new business. I look forward to participating in the rest of the interview process and to being a part of your team."

Don't assume the interviewer will connect all the dots. It is up to you to enlighten the interviewer on why there is a mutual benefit and why they should extend a job offer.

Straightforward Approach:
This approach is simple, clear-cut. Here's an example:

"I'm interested in the position. Have I provided all the information you need to offer me the position?"

By professionally asking for the job, you may be pleasantly surprised — they may offer it to you right on the spot!

By doing your homework prior to the interview, wearing your best interview clothes, and greeting your interviewer with a solid handshake, you are off to a solid start. By practicing mirroring techniques, getting permission from the interviewer to take notes, and asking well thought out questions about the company and the job, you are someone the interviewer will take seriously. Finally, by being likeable, smiling often, not discussing compensation, and asking for the job, you are creating an atmosphere where the interviewer will be taking you seriously for the job.

If the company does not hire you after the first interview, you are now on to the follow-up phase. This phase will be much easier if you are able to secure the hiring timeline as previously discussed.

FOLLOW UP 6

It's important to make sure your interviewers will remember you. Cement your image into their minds with a great first impression and a strong follow-up technique. According to www.about.com, only 10% of interviewees ever follow-up with a thank you letter. Not only will you look more professional but you'll stand out from the crowd. Pretty soon, they'll wonder how they ever survived without you!

Deciding what to send: Note or Letter?
There are distinct times when a thank you note is all that is needed, and other times where it is not enough. How do you know? On the other hand, when is a thank you letter overkill?

Thank you notes should be used when you have held a similar position many times before. They are short, generally 3-5 short sentences, and are written on a small thank you note card.

Address the interviewer by name, thanking them for the opportunity to meet with you on said date, for said position. Highlight one great skill you bring to the table, or asset you have (ability to start immediately, project management knowledge, excellent computer skills). Then end the note by restating your interest in the position.

Thank you letters are used for many reasons, such as to provide additional information or to clarify a concern addressed in the interview.

Here is a list of times when a follow-up letter is necessary:

- To address a concern raised in the interview
- To provide additional information
- After meeting a campus recruiter
- After a Career/Job Fair Interview
- When building up your strengths is needed
- When stressing your fit for the position is needed
- After meeting while Career Networking

Who do you send a Thank-you to?
It is better to give too much thanks than to forget to thank someone. Plan on sending a letter or note (as applicable) to each person who interviewed you directly. Also send thank you notes to your references and anyone who refers a job to you. Be sure to vary what you write to each person.

SEND A THANK YOU NOTE
If you can't do it before you leave the parking lot, be sure to do it within 24 hours of the interview. There are several reasons to send a thank you note (beyond the fact that it's just polite). If the interview went well, a note can reiterate to the interviewer why you feel you would be a great asset to their company, and keep you "on top" in their mind during the selection process.

Even if this particular job clearly is not for you, a thank you note still helps. It ends things positively, and shows you're professional and truly appreciate being considered for the job. If the interviewer likes you, but this job isn't a good fit, there's a chance that they might get back to you later with something better, or be willing to refer you to other people for other job openings that better fit your skills.

Another reason to send a thank-you note is that it makes you, the job seeker, feel psychologically positive. It's part of doing everything possible to secure the job. It helps to be able to think that you are doing another small step to find a job.

There are also several ways to send a thank you note... handwritten and mailed, by email, or by fax. I am a big believer that a handwritten thank you note shows greater sincerity than an email. The only time I suggest email is when a hiring decision is going to be made by the company within 24 to 48 hours of your interview. Even if there is a tight hiring timeline, you can always hand-deliver the thank you, to match the company's sense of hiring urgency.

FUNDAMENTALS OF A GENERAL THANK YOU LETTER

If the interview didn't go perfectly, writing a letter is another opportunity for you to maintain a professional, constructive conversation, and in a way, correct things you may think you said wrong. Some interviewers are intentionally hard on job seekers during the interview, as a way to "test" applicants. It doesn't necessarily mean they won't hire you. Following up after the interview can be a determining factor.

Here's an outline of what your thank you should look like:

First Paragraph
Use the first paragraph of your thank you letter to show your genuine appreciation for the job interview and to reinforce your interest and why you feel you are a great fit for the position. Use words like thank you, thanks, appreciate, excited, and enjoyed.

Example:
"Thank you so much for taking the time to discuss the assistant store manager position at ABC Co. with me. After meeting with you and the other members of the management team, I am further convinced that my

background and skills are perfect for the position."

Second Paragraph
Use the second paragraph to showcase some of the key elements of your background that match exactly what the employer is seeking. Use words like convinced, ability, experience, achieve, collaborate, and contribute.

Example:
"I am eager to bring my previous retail management experiences, strategic problem-solving skills and passion for your good name to your store. I am convinced the knowledge, skills, and experience I've already achieved make me the best candidate for the job."

Third Paragraph
Use this optional paragraph to reinforce a point you perceived as a possible weakness during the interview or to play up a key strength the employer seeks — or to mention something you forgot to state in the interview.

Example:
"As for your concern about my number of years of retail management experience, I want to reiterate that my having been new member recruitment chair at my school's chapter of the ARA, along with outstanding grades in my professional management classes, qualify me nicely."

Fourth Paragraph
The fourth and final paragraph of your thank you letter should again thank the interviewer for the interview and for being considered for the position, and mention that you are looking forward to the next step in the process and hearing back from him or her shortly.

Example:
"I look forward to hearing from you regarding your hiring decision. I know I am the perfect candidate for the position. Finally, thank you again for your time and consideration."

FINAL THOUGHTS

Remember, this formula is just an outline of a thank you letter. While the content is important, it's just as important to write it and get it into the interviewer's hands as quickly as possible. Listen to and write from your heart.

Of course, if you are offered the job the same day as the interview, send a thank you note for the interview and the job offer!

TELEPHONE FOLLOW-UP

If you have not heard back from the interviewer within the timeline you discussed and set up during the interview, or you were unable to get a timeline, a good rule of thumb is to call one day after your thank you note would have arrived. Normally, that would be three days after the interview, not counting weekends.

The call should reference two to three key points you took from the interview, and reinforce your interest in the position. It is important to use standard telephone etiquette. Do not call from your car, the bathroom, the mall, or the living room with the television blasting in the background. If you have to leave a voicemail or a message with a receptionist, be sure to speak clearly, cover the points listed above and, above all else, be professional and courteous.

Practice this script several times before calling and using it, or use it to build your own. It is important to sound clear and smooth but it is also important not to sound like you are reading something.

"Hello, Mr./Ms. _____, this is Bob Smith and I am following up on my recent interview with you regarding your open accountant position.

After meeting with you, I was hoping for the opportunity to talk with you more about why I feel I would be a good addition to your team. With over 10 years of experience in accounting, I know I could bring a positive impact to your team.

Please call me back at _____. If I don't hear back from you soon, I will call you back in 2 days. Thank you, and goodbye."

WHEN FAILURE HAPPENS

So you didn't get the job. It was bound to happen at some point. There are no guarantees when it comes to conducting a job search. Many of the factors that determine whether or not you will get the job are beyond your control. Sometimes the job you're perfect for goes to someone else, sometimes companies lose a client and then decide that they can't hire at that time, and sometimes you simply don't get the job because you are not the most qualified applicant. In the Job Search Process™ there will be highs and lows. You can count on it.

Many job seekers feel that the lowest point is when they do not get the job they really wanted or needed. Job seekers are often so disappointed by the news that they fail to find out exactly why they weren't chosen. By not asking why, they end up missing out on a golden learning opportunity.

WHY NOT ME?

As painful as it may be, you need to try to find out why you didn't get the job. This kind of criticism could have a necessary impact on the way you see yourself and the way you conduct yourself during interviews. The best way to find out why you weren't chosen, is to ask the hiring manager.

A simple statement such as, "I realize that I wasn't chosen for this job and I can accept that. What I would like from you is your help. Specifically, I would like to learn why I wasn't, and what suggested changes you may have for me for future interviews I go on, so that I can secure the employment that I need." Chances are, you will learn a great deal from the interviewer regarding what you could have done differently. This type of job coaching is extremely valuable.

When I graduated from college, I was one of three finalists for two positions in a retail management training program. I had gone through several rounds of interviews and thought I was going to be receiving a job offer any day. Instead, I received a call from the HR manager stating that I finished third. Two other candidates were chosen instead of me. I was devastated. I had recently gotten married and we had a baby on the way. I needed that job!

I gathered my thoughts, wrote down a few questions, and I called the hiring manager to find out why I wasn't chosen. I began the call by saying that I simply wanted to learn from the experience, and asked if he could he let me know where I was lacking in the interview process and what could I do to improve my technique. He was very gracious and talked with me at length about how I presented myself, the answers I gave that he liked, and the answers I gave that were less impressive. I thanked him for his candor and time and concluded the telephone call.

Three days later the hiring manager called to inform me that one of the two other candidates had declined the job offer and he wanted to extend that job offer to me. He said he was impressed that I called after not receiving a job offer, and considered that a good demonstration of character.

I cannot say for sure whether I would have received the job offer if I didn't call the hiring manager. I can say, however, that I felt I did everything possible to get what I could from the experience, and that I was pleasantly surprised to receive the job offer, which I accepted.

WHEN TO GIVE UP

There are no hard and fast rules regarding how many messages you should leave if the hiring manager never returns your calls. Typically, if you have sent a thank you note and left two to three messages and the company hasn't communicated with you, you probably did not get the job.

The fact is, if you didn't get the job, the hiring manager or HR representative feels that they are delivering "bad news" to you. People prefer to avoid giving bad news. Telling someone they did not get the job can be as tough for the person giving the message, as it is for the person hearing it.

While not often the case, you may hear from the company several weeks later with job offer. Just don't count on it.

DON'T LET A GREAT INTERVIEW INTERRUPT YOUR SEARCH

I cannot emphasize this point enough — DO NOT fall in love with one great interview experience! There are so many variables in the hiring process at most companies, many of which are beyond your control, that you have keep focused on your personal job search process.

Practically speaking, you do not have a job until the first day you arrive at work. Until then, you are still seeking the best job opportunity for you and your family. This requires a disciplined approach to the Job Search Process™. Often, the best part of this discipline is that many job candidates will end up with two to three job offers, and can then leverage one offer against another offer, resulting in the best job offer possible.

Let's assume that you have now received a preliminary job offer, dependent on reaching a compensation plan. This is when research and negotiation are key components to getting you this job.

NEGOTIATE THE SALARY YOU DESERVE

It's important to know what you're worth and know what someone is willing to pay you. There is often a gap between how much job seekers think they're worth, and how much they are actually worth. This comes from many sources, including the job seekers' own ego, what friends or family share about their own job experiences, organized union labor, and media opinions.

The reality is very simple — as a job seeker, you are worth what someone else is willing to pay you. It is your responsibility to demonstrate to them that you are worth the money you are seeking. In order to best demonstrate your value to a potential employer, that you will need to not only conduct a strong interview, you also need to have some additional market intelligence on your side.

KNOW WHAT'S REASONABLE IN YOUR NEIGHBORHOOD

Each region within the United States has a typical pay scale, per job category, based on several factors, including the local cost of living, how many people in your area have your same skillset, regional economic factors, and industry-specific economic factors. You will need to know what the current wages are for the work you do, based on where you live.

For example, if you worked as a laborer in an automobile factory in Detroit, you were accustomed to making a decent living with strong benefits. That employment landscape has quickly shifted downward in the Detroit auto market. Someone's $32 an job a decade ago, now pays $14 an hour, with decreased benefits.

If you are looking to relocate, use the internet to get an idea of what other regions around the United States are paying for your skills and talents. A good resource for that info is www.salary.com or www.salaryexpert.com. A note of caution, any website like salary.com, is based on a collection of data and should only be used a guide, not treated as 100% factual for every employer with which you interview.

SHARE YOUR HISTORY

A new trend amongst employers is to ask for a salary history from their job seekers, especially for managerial job openings. Candidates are now being asked to provide W-2 information to show the accuracy of what they say.

With people fabricating salary information, companies have stopped taking job seekers at their word. As long as you have been honest and accurate with your income numbers, providing this information in the form of a W-2 should be mere formality, instead of an insulting request.

BE WILLING TO PROVE YOURSELF

In the business world, similar to the professional sports world, companies occasionally want to see what you can do before they pay you as much as you were making previously.

If you are able to go into company and demonstrate your value, you will create a provable situation where you will then be able to ask for a raise.

As a recruiter, I have heard from many candidates about how great they are at their jobs, yet it can be difficult to tell which ones will actually perform. I have had several talented individuals work for a little less money when they first started their new jobs, in order to show employers how valuable they were. It has been my experience that great employees normally can get a raise within six months of starting a new job.

HOW TO NEGOTIATE

Sometimes the initial offer you receive from a company isn't the only offer available. You always have the option of counter-offering after you receive the first offer from the company. If you are able to create a reasonable, win-win request, they'll probably listen.

Negotiate to your strength. If you are a smooth talker (an extrovert), call the employer and ask for a follow-up meeting to discuss a counter-offer. If you communicate better in writing, follow our guidelines for writing a counter-proposal letter. Take a look at the example below.

Sample Counter Proposal Letter
(from Randall Hansen, PhD.)

While there is not a specific formula to writing a successful counter proposal letter, there is a basic structure you can follow for maximum likelihood of success.

First Paragraph:
Statement of Interest and Enthusiasm for Job/Company; Key Selling Factors.

This paragraph is critical in setting up the tone and direction of the negotiations. Be direct and sincere in expressing your interest for the company, thanking the employer for the job offer. Be sure to follow-up with your key selling points — how you will make a direct and immediate (or longer-term) impact on the organization.

Second Paragraph:
Negotiating Item #1 — Offer and Counter Proposal

Restate the particular point from the original offer that you wish to negotiate, followed by your counter proposal — ideally supported through research, a desire to be fairly compensated, or reinforced by the value you will bring to the company.

Third Paragraph:
Negotiating Item #2 — Offer and Counter Proposal

Restate the particular point from the original offer that you wish to negotiate, followed by your counter proposal — ideally supported through research, a desire to be fairly compensated, or reinforced by the value you will bring to the company. You could repeat this formula for as many items as you wish to counter.

Concluding Paragraph:
Conciliatory Comments with Strong Moving-Forward Statement.

Stress that your requests are modest and that your potential impact is great; that you look forward to accepting the offered position, and to getting a jump-start on the job as soon as possible.

You can also include paragraphs for items of the original

proposal that you completely agree on, to make the letter seem more balanced. If you need any further explanation on anything, you should also include paragraphs for any items in the offer that need clarification, typically for complex issues such as confidentiality, non-compete agreements, and bonus plans.

Always ask for a higher salary or hourly wage (within acceptable limits) than you are willing to accept, so that when the employer counters your proposal, the salary or hourly wage should be near your original goal. When possible, try to show how your actions (once you are hired) will recoup the extra amount (or more) that you are seeking. Show them how you are going to do this through cost savings or increased sales revenue, productivity, and efficiencies.

If the salary/hourly wage you're offered is on the low end — and the employer has stated that the salary/hourly wage is not negotiable (probably due to corporate salary ranges/ hourly wage or pay grade levels), consider negotiating for a signing bonus, higher performance bonuses, or a shorter time frame for a performance review and raise. Always negotiate base salary/hourly wage first, and then move on to other elements of the job offer.

Never stop selling yourself throughout the negotiation process. Keep reminding the employer of the impact you will make, the problems you will solve, the revenue you will generate. And continue expressing interest and enthusiasm for the job and the company. Never make demands. Instead, ask questions and make requests during negotiations. Keep the tone conversational, not confrontational.

Be aware, however, that just because you are trying to negotiate with the company doesn't mean they will always negotiate with you. Currently, there are more job seekers than there are jobs. You run the risk of appearing to be out of touch with the company's perception of their current economic conditions or the employment marketplace conditions. The company may have several candidates and could take back the offer they made to you and give it to a job seeker that is willing to accept the first offer.

It's important to remember that a compensation package is more than just salary/hourly wage. Other pieces, such as health benefits and their accompanying co-pays, vacation/personal time off, 401(k) contributions and other miscellaneous expenses incurred by the company should all be taken into consideration as well.

WHEN TO WALK AWAY

The ideal time to walk away from a frustrating negotiation is when you have another job offer. If you don't have another job offer, but the offer from the company is completely below your market value, and they are unable or unwilling to negotiate, you should thank them for the offer, politely inform them that you will not be accepting at this time.

Always leave an offer on the table professionally and positively. In strong economic times, there have been many occasions when a company will approach a job candidate a second time, after their "final offer" has been rejected. Remember, it's nothing personal, it's business.

After some professional negotiations, you and the employer have finally reached an understanding on your compensation plan. All of your hours of hard work, your willingness to follow and trust in the Job Search Process™ have finally paid off. You have now secured a job you are pleased with. You tell your family and friends about your new job opportunity and they share in your positive excitement. Celebrate your hard earned success!

At this stage, most people think their work is done — simply show up, put your time in and you are secure for the time being. WRONG!! Now it's time to show your worth as a valuable employee and prove to your employer that they made the right decision hiring you.

START YOUR NEW JOB WITH A BANG!

It's important to your success with your new company to create a lasting first impression on your boss and your co-workers. Candidates often believe that once they have accepted a new job, their work is done. Nothing could be farther from the truth.

As long as you are with the company, your attitude and performance will be under the microscope. As the global economy rises and falls like an uncertain ocean tide, companies are scrutinizing their personnel more than ever before.

With layoffs now being determined not entirely by seniority, but by productivity and skillset, beware of an employer who has to get more work done with a smaller headcount. Unless you want to be looking for a job at the decision of corporate management, you will want to be a productive, competent team player beginning on your first day.

20 Tips for New Job Impressions:
1. Have a positive attitude
2. Dress professionally, to blend in with co-workers
3. Show your team spirit
4. Learn co-workers' names quickly
5. Ask questions, and ask for help
6. Take notes/go to orientation
7. Be a self-starter/take initiative
8. Discover everything about your new employer
9. Work full days
10. Establish a good attendance record
11. Avoid office politics and gossip
12. Keep personal business on company time to a minimum
13. Take advantage of after-hours activities
14. Listen more than talk
15. Track accomplishments
16. Show appreciation
17. Find a mentor
18. Get and stay organized/set goals
19. Keep your boss informed — of everything
20. Meet and network with key people in your organization and profession

BE AN "AND THEN SOME" EMPLOYEE

Whether it's in writing or not, everyone has a job description. It includes their responsibilities, what they need to accomplish, and how they are measured.

People often treat that job description as a guidebook for what it takes to get a raise or as guidelines on how to move up within a company. Most people have it all wrong.

The people who move up in a company are the "and then some…" employees. These are the workers that do their job and then take on more work and responsibility. They are the first ones to volunteer to help a co-worker on a project, to come in early or stay late to meet an important customer deadline. They exceed sales quotas. They do their jobs — and then some.

If you want to move up in the company or make more money, make yourself valuable, by coming in early, staying late, doing work others don't want to do, and making a difference. Simply doing the basics of your job, and expecting that to get you raises or promotions, is no longer good enough.

BONUS STEP: THE LAST-DITCH EFFORT 9

(Recommended for Dream Jobs Only)

If you find your dream job and you cannot get the company to commit to hiring you, don't give up. You still have one shot at landing the job. It's risky, but extremely powerful and often career changing.

If, after doing all of your research on the company, sitting through the interview process, meeting and interacting with your potential supervisor and co-workers, you are absolutely convinced that you are the perfect fit for this company and vice-versa, offer to work for them for FREE for 2 weeks*. Similar to an unpaid college internship or commission only sales position, you would need to set up guidelines, goals and objectives to hit, and a final performance review after the two week period.

In 12 years of recruiting, I can honestly say that I have never seen a company turn down the person who offers to work for them for free. It is a bold statement made by the job seeker that shows commitment and a high level of interest in joining an organization.

Should the employer reject your offer, you have lost absolutely nothing, since you didn't have the job to begin with.

*Before committing this program, be sure to check with your state or federal tax advisor, regarding applicable state and federal laws.

CONCLUSION

It is my sincere intent that you will have found empowerment and hope in reading The Job Search Process™ and that you will be inspired to follow the process as it is outlined. I realize that it takes a great deal of hard work and effort to find a new job — from the hours of research, to writing your resume, sending it out and following up on its status. From time-consuming interview prep to the stress of the actual interview, all followed by more follow-up processes and then finally the job offer and compensation negation...

This is definitely not easy.

I commend you for your faith in using The Job Search Process™, and I would love the chance to hear your success stories of securing a new job for you and your family. Please feel free to share your stories with me at tpalmer@jobsearchprocess.com.

MY PLANNER

The planner portion of this book will help you follow our step-by-step process to finding a job. Allow this to be your guide and planner as you begin your search. Remember to relax, have fun and show your confidence!

Let's get started!

QUESTIONS TO ASK YOURSELF

Here are a couple questions Todd recommends you answer before beginning your search:

Who am I, really, and what do I have to offer to a new company?

_____

_____

_____

_____

_____

_____

What am I looking for in my next job?

_____

_____

_____

_____

_____

What will I need to do to get that job, and can I commit to doing whatever it takes?

_____

_____

_____

_____

_____

_____

MY DREAM JOB

_____

_____

_____

_____

_____

_____

_____

_____

_____

_____

_____

_____

_____

_____

_____

_____

_____

_____

_____

_____

_____

_____

_____

MY VISION

If nothing else mattered...

These are my dreams, goals and aspirations. THINK BIG!

_____

_____

_____

_____

_____

_____

_____

_____

_____

_____

_____

_____

_____

_____

_____

_____

_____

_____

_____

_____

_____

_____

MY PERSONAL MISSION STATEMENT

Take control of your personal life!

_____

_____

_____

_____

_____

_____

_____

_____

_____

_____

_____

_____

_____

_____

_____

_____

_____

_____

_____

_____

_____

_____

_____

_____

_____

_____

_____

_____

_____

MY CAREER
MISSION STATEMENT

Take control of your career!

_____

_____

_____

_____

_____

_____

_____

_____

_____

_____

_____

_____

_____

_____

_____

_____

_____

_____

_____

_____

_____

_____

_____

_____

MY TOP 5 TRANSFERABLE SKILLS

List your top five skills and other places they could be used.

Skill 1

_____

_____

_____

Skill 2

_____

_____

_____

Skill 3

_____

_____

_____

Skill 4

_____

_____

_____

Skill 5

_____

_____

_____

MY SUPPORT SYSTEM

**List the names and contact information of the people who will always
be there to support you and keep you positive during your job search**

Name	Phone	Email

REWARDS

Make a list of some of the items you are saving up for when you have achieved something deserving of a small personal reward.

_____

_____

_____

_____

_____

_____

_____

_____

_____

_____

_____

_____

_____

_____

_____

_____

_____

_____

_____

_____

WEEK ONE

Start by planning your week

This week, I want to:

_____

_____

_____

_____

This week, I need to:

_____

_____

_____

_____

Daily goals for this week:

_____

_____

_____

_____

Resume Goal:

_____

_____

Interview Goal:

_____

_____

_____

MY DAILY PLAN
DAY ONE

It's a new day…

Today's Date:

_____

To do today:

_____

_____

_____

Evening plans:

_____

_____

Today's accomplishments:

_____

_____

Book I'm reading:

_____

_____

Exercise:

_____

_____

Number of resumes:

_____

Calls to make:

_____

_____

MY DAILY PLAN
DAY TWO

It's a new day…

Today's Date:

_____

To do today:

_____

_____

_____

Evening plans:

_____

_____

Today's accomplishments:

_____

_____

Book I'm reading:

_____

_____

Exercise:

_____

_____

Number of resumes:

_____

Calls to make:

_____

_____

MY DAILY PLAN
DAY THREE

It's a new day…

Today's Date:

_____

To do today:

_____

_____

_____

Evening plans:

_____

_____

Today's accomplishments:

_____

_____

Book I'm reading:

_____

_____

Exercise:

_____

_____

Number of resumes:

_____

Calls to make:

_____

_____

MY DAILY PLAN
DAY FOUR

It's a new day…

Today's Date:

_____

To do today:

_____

_____

_____

Evening plans:

_____

_____

Today's accomplishments:

_____

_____

Book I'm reading:

_____

_____

Exercise:

_____

_____

Number of resumes:

_____

Calls to make:

_____

_____

MY DAILY PLAN
DAY FIVE

It's a new day…

Today's Date:

_____

To do today:

_____

_____

_____

Evening plans:

_____

_____

Today's accomplishments:

_____

_____

Book I'm reading:

_____

_____

Exercise:

_____

_____

Number of resumes:

_____

Calls to make:

_____

_____

MY DAILY PLAN
DAY SIX

It's a new day…

Today's Date:

_____

To do today:

_____

_____

_____

Evening plans:

_____

_____

Today's accomplishments:

_____

_____

Book I'm reading:

_____

_____

Exercise:

_____

_____

Number of resumes:

_____

Calls to make:

_____

_____

MY DAILY PLAN
DAY SEVEN

It's a new day…

Today's Date:

_____

To do today:

_____

_____

_____

Evening plans:

_____

_____

Today's accomplishments:

_____

_____

Book I'm reading:

_____

_____

Exercise:

_____

_____

Number of resumes:

_____

Calls to make:

_____

_____

WEEK TWO

Start by planning your week

This week, I want to:

_____
_____
_____
_____

This week, I need to:

_____
_____
_____
_____

Daily goals for this week:

_____
_____
_____
_____

Resume Goal:

_____
_____
_____

Interview Goal:

_____
_____
_____

MY DAILY PLAN
DAY ONE

It's a new day…

Today's Date:

_____

To do today:

_____

_____

_____

Evening plans:

_____

_____

Today's accomplishments:

_____

_____

Book I'm reading:

_____

_____

Exercise:

_____

_____

Number of resumes:

_____

Calls to make:

_____

_____

MY DAILY PLAN
DAY TWO

It's a new day…

Today's Date:

_____

To do today:

_____

_____

_____

Evening plans:

_____

_____

Today's accomplishments:

_____

_____

Book I'm reading:

_____

_____

Exercise:

_____

_____

Number of resumes:

_____

Calls to make:

_____

_____

MY DAILY PLAN
DAY THREE

It's a new day…

Today's Date:

_____

To do today:

_____

_____

_____

Evening plans:

_____

_____

Today's accomplishments:

_____

_____

Book I'm reading:

_____

_____

Exercise:

_____

_____

Number of resumes:

_____

Calls to make:

_____

_____

MY DAILY PLAN
DAY FOUR

It's a new day…

Today's Date:

_____

To do today:

_____

_____

_____

Evening plans:

_____

_____

Today's accomplishments:

_____

_____

Book I'm reading:

_____

_____

Exercise:

_____

_____

Number of resumes:

_____

Calls to make:

_____

_____

MY DAILY PLAN
DAY FIVE

It's a new day…

Today's Date:

_____

To do today:

_____

_____

_____

Evening plans:

_____

_____

Today's accomplishments:

_____

_____

Book I'm reading:

_____

_____

Exercise:

_____

_____

Number of resumes:

_____

Calls to make:

_____

_____

MY DAILY PLAN
DAY SIX

It's a new day…

Today's Date:

_____

To do today:

_____

_____

_____

Evening plans:

_____

_____

Today's accomplishments:

_____

_____

Book I'm reading:

_____

_____

Exercise:

_____

_____

Number of resumes:

_____

Calls to make:

_____

_____

MY DAILY PLAN
DAY SEVEN

It's a new day…

Today's Date:

_____

To do today:

_____

_____

_____

Evening plans:

_____

_____

Today's accomplishments:

_____

_____

Book I'm reading:

_____

_____

Exercise:

_____

_____

Number of resumes:

_____

Calls to make:

_____

_____

WEEK THREE

Start by planning your week

This week, I want to:

_____

_____

_____

_____

This week, I need to:

_____

_____

_____

_____

Daily goals for this week:

_____

_____

_____

_____

Resume Goal:

_____

_____

Interview Goal:

_____

_____

_____

MY DAILY PLAN
DAY ONE

It's a new day…

Today's Date:

_____

To do today:

_____

_____

_____

Evening plans:

_____

_____

Today's accomplishments:

_____

_____

Book I'm reading:

_____

_____

Exercise:

_____

_____

Number of resumes:

_____

Calls to make:

_____

_____

MY DAILY PLAN
DAY TWO

It's a new day...

Today's Date:

_____

To do today:

_____

_____

_____

Evening plans:

_____

_____

Today's accomplishments:

_____

_____

Book I'm reading:

_____

_____

Exercise:

_____

_____

Number of resumes:

_____

Calls to make:

_____

_____

MY DAILY PLAN
DAY THREE

It's a new day…

Today's Date:

_____

To do today:

_____

_____

_____

Evening plans:

_____

_____

Today's accomplishments:

_____

_____

Book I'm reading:

_____

_____

Exercise:

_____

_____

Number of resumes:

_____

Calls to make:

_____

_____

MY DAILY PLAN
DAY FOUR

It's a new day…

Today's Date:

_____

To do today:

_____

_____

_____

Evening plans:

_____

_____

Today's accomplishments:

_____

_____

Book I'm reading:

_____

_____

Exercise:

_____

_____

Number of resumes:

_____

Calls to make:

_____

_____

MY DAILY PLAN
DAY FIVE

It's a new day…

Today's Date:

_____

To do today:

_____

_____

_____

Evening plans:

_____

_____

Today's accomplishments:

_____

_____

Book I'm reading:

_____

_____

Exercise:

_____

_____

Number of resumes:

_____

Calls to make:

_____

_____

MY DAILY PLAN
DAY SIX

It's a new day…

Today's Date:

_____

To do today:

_____

_____

_____

Evening plans:

_____

_____

Today's accomplishments:

_____

_____

Book I'm reading:

_____

_____

Exercise:

_____

_____

Number of resumes:

_____

Calls to make:

_____

_____

MY DAILY PLAN
DAY SEVEN

It's a new day…

Today's Date:

_____

To do today:

_____

_____

_____

Evening plans:

_____

_____

Today's accomplishments:

_____

_____

Book I'm reading:

_____

_____

Exercise:

_____

_____

Number of resumes:

_____

Calls to make:

_____

_____

WEEK FOUR

Start by planning your week

This week, I want to:

_____

_____

_____

_____

This week, I need to:

_____

_____

_____

_____

Daily goals for this week:

_____

_____

_____

_____

Resume Goal:

_____

_____

_____

Interview Goal:

_____

_____

_____

MY DAILY PLAN
DAY ONE

It's a new day...

Today's Date:

_____

To do today:

_____

_____

_____

Evening plans:

_____

_____

Today's accomplishments:

_____

_____

Book I'm reading:

_____

_____

Exercise:

_____

_____

Number of resumes:

_____

Calls to make:

_____

_____

MY DAILY PLAN
DAY TWO

It's a new day…

Today's Date:

_____

To do today:

_____

_____

_____

Evening plans:

_____

_____

Today's accomplishments:

_____

_____

Book I'm reading:

_____

_____

Exercise:

_____

_____

Number of resumes:

_____

Calls to make:

_____

_____

MY DAILY PLAN
DAY THREE

It's a new day…

Today's Date:

_____

To do today:

_____

_____

_____

Evening plans:

_____

_____

Today's accomplishments:

_____

_____

Book I'm reading:

_____

_____

Exercise:

_____

_____

Number of resumes:

_____

Calls to make:

_____

_____

MY DAILY PLAN
DAY FOUR

It's a new day…

Today's Date:

_____

To do today:

_____

_____

_____

Evening plans:

_____

_____

Today's accomplishments:

_____

_____

Book I'm reading:

_____

_____

Exercise:

_____

_____

Number of resumes:

_____

Calls to make:

_____

_____

MY DAILY PLAN
DAY FIVE

It's a new day…

Today's Date:

_____

To do today:

_____

_____

_____

Evening plans:

_____

_____

Today's accomplishments:

_____

_____

Book I'm reading:

_____

_____

Exercise:

_____

_____

Number of resumes:

_____

Calls to make:

_____

_____

MY DAILY PLAN
DAY SIX

It's a new day…

Today's Date:

_____

To do today:

_____

_____

_____

Evening plans:

_____

_____

Today's accomplishments:

_____

_____

Book I'm reading:

_____

_____

Exercise:

_____

_____

Number of resumes:

_____

Calls to make:

_____

_____

MY DAILY PLAN
DAY SEVEN

It's a new day...

Today's Date:

_____

To do today:

_____

_____

_____

Evening plans:

_____

_____

Today's accomplishments:

_____

_____

Book I'm reading:

_____

_____

Exercise:

_____

_____

Number of resumes:

_____

Calls to make:

_____

_____

WEEK FIVE

Start by planning your week

This week, I want to:

_____
_____
_____
_____

This week, I need to:

_____
_____
_____
_____

Daily goals for this week:

_____
_____
_____
_____

Resume Goal:

_____
_____
_____

Interview Goal:

_____
_____
_____

MY DAILY PLAN
DAY ONE

It's a new day…

Today's Date:

_____

To do today:

_____

_____

_____

Evening plans:

_____

_____

Today's accomplishments:

_____

_____

Book I'm reading:

_____

_____

Exercise:

_____

_____

Number of resumes:

_____

Calls to make:

_____

_____

MY DAILY PLAN
DAY TWO

It's a new day…

Today's Date:

_____

To do today:

_____

_____

_____

Evening plans:

_____

_____

Today's accomplishments:

_____

_____

Book I'm reading:

_____

_____

Exercise:

_____

_____

Number of resumes:

_____

Calls to make:

_____

_____

MY DAILY PLAN
DAY THREE

It's a new day…

Today's Date:

_____

To do today:

_____

_____

_____

Evening plans:

_____

_____

Today's accomplishments:

_____

_____

Book I'm reading:

_____

_____

Exercise:

_____

_____

Number of resumes:

_____

Calls to make:

_____

_____

MY DAILY PLAN
DAY FOUR

It's a new day…

Today's Date:

_____

To do today:

_____

_____

_____

Evening plans:

_____

_____

Today's accomplishments:

_____

_____

Book I'm reading:

_____

_____

Exercise:

_____

_____

Number of resumes:

_____

Calls to make:

_____

_____

MY DAILY PLAN
DAY FIVE

It's a new day…

Today's Date:

_____

To do today:

_____

_____

_____

Evening plans:

_____

_____

Today's accomplishments:

_____

_____

Book I'm reading:

_____

_____

Exercise:

_____

_____

Number of resumes:

_____

Calls to make:

_____

_____

MY DAILY PLAN
DAY SIX

It's a new day…

Today's Date:

_____

To do today:

_____

_____

_____

Evening plans:

_____

_____

Today's accomplishments:

_____

_____

Book I'm reading:

_____

_____

Exercise:

_____

_____

Number of resumes:

_____

Calls to make:

_____

_____

MY DAILY PLAN
DAY SEVEN

It's a new day…

Today's Date:

_____

To do today:

_____

_____

_____

Evening plans:

_____

_____

Today's accomplishments:

_____

_____

Book I'm reading:

_____

_____

Exercise:

_____

_____

Number of resumes:

_____

Calls to make:

_____

_____

WEEK SIX

Start by planning your week

This week, I want to:

_____

_____

_____

_____

This week, I need to:

_____

_____

_____

_____

Daily goals for this week:

_____

_____

_____

_____

Resume Goal:

_____

_____

_____

Interview Goal:

_____

_____

_____

MY DAILY PLAN
DAY ONE

It's a new day…

Today's Date:

_____

To do today:

_____

_____

_____

Evening plans:

_____

_____

Today's accomplishments:

_____

_____

Book I'm reading:

_____

_____

Exercise:

_____

_____

Number of resumes:

_____

Calls to make:

_____

_____

MY DAILY PLAN
DAY TWO

It's a new day...

Today's Date:

_____

To do today:

_____

_____

_____

Evening plans:

_____

_____

Today's accomplishments:

_____

_____

Book I'm reading:

_____

_____

Exercise:

_____

_____

Number of resumes:

_____

Calls to make:

_____

_____

MY DAILY PLAN
DAY THREE

It's a new day…

Today's Date:

_____

To do today:

_____

_____

_____

Evening plans:

_____

_____

Today's accomplishments:

_____

_____

Book I'm reading:

_____

_____

Exercise:

_____

_____

Number of resumes:

_____

Calls to make:

_____

_____

MY DAILY PLAN
DAY FOUR

It's a new day…

Today's Date:

_____

To do today:

_____

_____

_____

Evening plans:

_____

_____

Today's accomplishments:

_____

_____

Book I'm reading:

_____

_____

Exercise:

_____

_____

Number of resumes:

_____

Calls to make:

_____

_____

MY DAILY PLAN
DAY FIVE

It's a new day...

Today's Date:

_____

To do today:

_____

_____

_____

Evening plans:

_____

_____

Today's accomplishments:

_____

_____

Book I'm reading:

_____

_____

Exercise:

_____

_____

Number of resumes:

_____

Calls to make:

_____

_____

MY DAILY PLAN
DAY SIX

It's a new day...

Today's Date:

_____

To do today:

_____

_____

_____

Evening plans:

_____

_____

Today's accomplishments:

_____

_____

Book I'm reading:

_____

_____

Exercise:

_____

_____

Number of resumes:

_____

Calls to make:

_____

_____

MY DAILY PLAN
DAY SEVEN

It's a new day…

Today's Date:

_____

To do today:

_____

_____

_____

Evening plans:

_____

_____

Today's accomplishments:

_____

_____

Book I'm reading:

_____

_____

Exercise:

_____

_____

Number of resumes:

_____

Calls to make:

_____

_____

WEEK SIX

Start by planning your week

This week, I want to:

_____

_____

_____

_____

This week, I need to:

_____

_____

_____

_____

Daily goals for this week:

_____

_____

_____

_____

Resume Goal:

_____

_____

_____

Interview Goal:

_____

_____

_____

MY DAILY PLAN
DAY ONE

It's a new day…

Today's Date:

_____

To do today:

_____

_____

_____

Evening plans:

_____

_____

Today's accomplishments:

_____

_____

Book I'm reading:

_____

_____

Exercise:

_____

_____

Number of resumes:

_____

Calls to make:

_____

_____

MY DAILY PLAN
DAY TWO

It's a new day…

Today's Date:

_____

To do today:

_____

_____

_____

Evening plans:

_____

_____

Today's accomplishments:

_____

_____

Book I'm reading:

_____

_____

Exercise:

_____

_____

Number of resumes:

_____

Calls to make:

_____

_____

MY DAILY PLAN
DAY THREE

It's a new day…

Today's Date:

_____

To do today:

_____

_____

_____

Evening plans:

_____

_____

Today's accomplishments:

_____

_____

Book I'm reading:

_____

_____

Exercise:

_____

_____

Number of resumes:

_____

Calls to make:

_____

_____

MY DAILY PLAN
DAY FOUR

It's a new day…

Today's Date:

_____

To do today:

_____

_____

_____

Evening plans:

_____

_____

Today's accomplishments:

_____

_____

Book I'm reading:

_____

_____

Exercise:

_____

_____

Number of resumes:

_____

Calls to make:

_____

_____

MY DAILY PLAN
DAY FIVE

It's a new day…

Today's Date:

_____

To do today:

_____

_____

_____

Evening plans:

_____

_____

Today's accomplishments:

_____

_____

Book I'm reading:

_____

_____

Exercise:

_____

_____

Number of resumes:

_____

Calls to make:

_____

_____

MY DAILY PLAN
DAY SIX

It's a new day...

Today's Date:

_____

To do today:

_____

_____

_____

Evening plans:

_____

_____

Today's accomplishments:

_____

_____

Book I'm reading:

_____

_____

Exercise:

_____

_____

Number of resumes:

_____

Calls to make:

_____

_____

COMPANY CHEAT SHEET

Company Name:

_____

What they do:

_____

_____

_____

Competitors:

_____

_____

Customers:

_____

_____

Media exposure:

_____

_____

Staff/management:

_____

_____

Other job openings:

_____

Expansion plans:

_____

_____

COMPANY CHEAT SHEET

Company Name:

_____

What they do:

_____

_____

_____

Competitors:

_____

_____

Customers:

_____

_____

Media exposure:

_____

_____

Staff/management:

_____

_____

Other job openings:

_____

Expansion plans:

_____

_____

COMPANY CHEAT SHEET

Company Name:

_____

What they do:

_____

_____

_____

Competitors:

_____

_____

Customers:

_____

_____

Media exposure:

_____

_____

Staff/management:

_____

_____

Other job openings:

_____

Expansion plans:

_____

_____

COMPANY
CHEAT SHEET

Company Name:

_____

What they do:

_____

_____

_____

Competitors:

_____

_____

Customers:

_____

_____

Media exposure:

_____

_____

Staff/management:

_____

_____

Other job openings:

_____

Expansion plans:

_____

_____

COMPANY CHEAT SHEET

Company Name:

_____

What they do:

_____

_____

_____

Competitors:

_____

_____

Customers:

_____

_____

Media exposure:

_____

_____

Staff/management:

_____

_____

Other job openings:

_____

Expansion plans:

_____

_____

COMPANY
CHEAT SHEET

Company Name:

_____

What they do:

_____

_____

_____

Competitors:

_____

_____

Customers:

_____

_____

Media exposure:

_____

_____

Staff/management:

_____

_____

Other job openings:

_____

Expansion plans:

_____

_____

COMPANY CHEAT SHEET

Company Name:

_____

What they do:

_____

_____

Competitors:

_____

Customers:

_____

Media exposure:

_____

Staff/management:

_____

Other job openings:

_____

Expansion plans:

_____

_____

COMPANY CHEAT SHEET

Company Name:

_____

What they do:

_____

_____

_____

Competitors:

_____

_____

Customers:

_____

_____

Media exposure:

_____

_____

Staff/management:

_____

_____

Other job openings:

_____

Expansion plans:

_____

_____

COMPANY CHEAT SHEET

Company Name:

_____

What they do:

_____

_____

_____

Competitors:

_____

_____

Customers:

_____

_____

Media exposure:

_____

_____

Staff/management:

_____

_____

Other job openings:

_____

Expansion plans:

_____

_____

COMPANY CHEAT SHEET

Company Name:

_____

What they do:

_____

_____

_____

Competitors:

_____

_____

Customers:

_____

_____

Media exposure:

_____

_____

Staff/management:

_____

_____

Other job openings:

_____

Expansion plans:

_____

_____

TODD PALMER

AUTHOR

Made in the USA
Monee, IL
31 August 2020